Norse Magic for Beginners

Beginners

THE ESSENTIAL GUIDE TO ELDER FUTHARK RUNES READING, NORSE DIVINATION, RITUALS, SPELLS, AND SYMBOLS

FRANK BAWDOE

CONTENTS

Thank you for adding this book to your Wiccan Library! To learn more, join Frank's Wiccan Community and get this additional free **Little Book of Magic Spells 100% FREE!**

    Little Book of Magic Spells is a great starting point for beginners looking to try their hand at practicing magic spells. It includes **19 beginner-friendly spells** that can help you create a positive atmosphere within your home, protect yourself from negativity, improve your overall health, attract love and prosperity.

    Hundreds of others are already enjoying insider access to all of my current and future full-length books, 100% free!

    If you want insider access plus this **free Little Book of Magic Spells,** all you have to do is **scan the QR code below** with your smartphone to claim your offer!

INTRODUCTION

You may not realize it, but Norse magic is all around you. I don't mean physically all around you - although it is true that once you've learned how to access magic, you'll likely find that you can do so almost anywhere. However, I'm referring to something a bit more mundane. I'm referring to the way that Norse culture has been woven into our own culture so thoroughly that many of us are likely unaware of its origins. There are some obvious examples, of course. Most of us probably know that the Marvel comics and movies took Thor and his magic hammer from Norse mythology (as well as Loki, Odin, Hela, the rainbow bridge, and many other things).

We may be less familiar with how Norse magic has found its way into other well-known stories, such as The Lord of the Rings books and films. Tolkien's pantheon of gods and demi-gods was heavily inspired by Norse mythology, just as his invented languages were inspired by actual Germanic languages. The Prose Edda, an ancient Icelandic text, was a major influence on Tolkien's work, from names to plot points to the setting itself. (Tolkien's "middle earth" is just a translation of "midgard", the Norse name for the realm of men.)

The Lord of the Rings and Marvel's Thor are just two prominent illustrations of Norse culture permeating modern pop culture. There are many more books and films that show evidence of Norse culture's impact, whether through overt retellings or more subtle inclusions. We also use bits of Norse mythology in everyday life - almost literally every day, in fact, since our names for Tuesday, Wednesday, Thursday, and Friday all come from the names of Norse deities. Even the ancient Norse writing system has found its way into modern life - whenever you hit the Bluetooth icon on your phone, you're looking at Norse runes.

Although it's fascinating to observe the fragments of the ancient Norse world that have embedded themselves into our current lives, these bits and pieces only hint at the depth and breadth of both that ancient world and the modern traditions that exist because of it. I suspect you might have picked this book up because at some point you've wondered if there was something more to these stories. Maybe you've felt a strong connection to the old Norse gods and their stories, a connection you can't quite explain. Maybe you've sensed there's something deeper waiting for you down this path. Or maybe you're just curious - which is great, because this book is here to answer all your questions.

WHAT YOU'LL LEARN FROM THIS BOOK

Like the nine realms of Norse mythology, this book also has nine parts. The first three chapters of the book will go over the history behind the Norse magic you'll be practicing, including:

- a brief overview of ancient Norse culture, where Norse magical practices first began - we'll discuss what the ancient Norse people believed, what we know about how they practiced these beliefs, and what we don't know because those beliefs were stamped out or driven underground with the advent of Christianity

- a quick introduction to the Norse pantheon of deities and the stories which shaped both ancient and modern Norse religious practices - we'll also cover elements such as the world tree and the nine realms, as well as the main gods which were and continue to be venerated in the practice of Norse magic
- a synopsis of the development of modern Norse religious practices, explaining how Norse religion made a comeback starting in the 1700s, and has continued to grow in popularity until the present day

The next three chapters will focus on the Norse magical practices themselves. These chapters will cover:

- a more in-depth discussion of Asatru, and other paths of Norse spirituality, as well as some of the key philosophical ideas of Norse ideology such as the nine noble virtues, frith, and wyrd
- Norse magical rituals (called "blóts") as well as other practices such as deity veneration, ancestor veneration, Norse pagan holidays, and spells
- an overview of symbols from Norse history, mythology, and religion, including well-known symbols such as Thor's hammer Mjölnir and Yggdrasil the tree of life, as well as more obscure symbols such as the Vegvisir (the "pointer of the way") and the Svefnthorn (the "sleep thorn")

The last three chapters will focus specifically on Norse runes and the ways they can be used for magical purposes. In these chapters you will gain:

- a solid background in the fascinating history of Norse runes, including their origins, what they mean, the philosophy behind them, and different ways they were used throughout ancient and modern history

- practical guidance on how to use Norse runes in your magic, with a deeper look at the magical element of runes, including how to incorporate them into your own rituals and spells, how to use them for binding spells, and how to make your own set of runes
- knowledge of different methods of divining the future in Norse history and modern magical practices, including learning about the ancient Seidr priestesses that were known for their prophecies, as well as how to practice divination by casting lots and rune casting

All of that may seem like a lot, but don't worry - we'll go through it one step at a time. My practice of Norse magic has given me a sense of agency and connection that I was unable to find in other religious traditions, but when I first started this journey I was overwhelmed. This book is the kind of clear, informative, and (hopefully) entertaining resource that I wish I'd had back then. I'm excited to take you on a journey of discovery - let's get started!

CHAPTER 1
EDDAS AND BLÓTS

Picture this: Northern Europe in the early middle ages, a cold and open place near the top of the world, populated by a people that history would remember for its fierce seafaring warriors and the epic tales of their daring adventures. It is not a place known for weakness or mercy, but somehow an idea of nobility and honor still hangs in the air. It's easy to picture, isn't it? Our imaginations have been captured by Norse history and its Vikings for a very long time, as evidenced by the way elements of that history have been absorbed into our modern world, as we just discussed in the introduction. But where did these ideas come from? And what do we really know about the early Norse people, the society they lived in, and the magic they practiced?

Medieval Norse society, like many others at the time, was built around local social structures, rather than a widespread central culture. Therefore pagan practitioners did not have religious organizations or institutions, as we might think of with churches and official religious denominations today. Instead, each region or tribe had specific practices that would have varied from place to place. These practices were not often written down, as the Norse peoples used oral traditions of information storing and sharing, rather than written. We know from archeological evidence found in graves and other sites that religion formed a large part of the ancient Norse way of life, but reconstructing exactly how that religion was practiced is harder. (Wilkes, 2021)

Therefore, remember as you read through this chapter that we're drawing a picture in broad strokes. We'll look at what we *do* know - and also a little bit about what we can't know and why.

WHAT'S AN EDDA?

I've already mentioned the Prose Edda, an inspiration to J.R.R. Tolkien, and a major source of information on Norse mythology. The Prose Edda was written around 1220 CE by an Icelandic poet and historian named Snorri Sturluson. (Lin, 2017) The Prose Edda was Snorri's most famous work, and it claimed to tell the story of the entire lifespan of the Norse world (or "midgard", as the Norse called it), from how it began to how it would end. Snorri was a practitioner of Christianity, writing about a time that was over before he was born - so it is not a firsthand account, and by no means can be considered infallible or always accurate. However, it is the most detailed and well-known account of Norse mythology and the religious practices of the Norse people. (Wilkes, 2021)

The origins of the name "Edda" are not known. Snorri used the word in another poem, where it referred to a "great-grandmother"; it is possible this term became associated with Snorri, and then later with the work he was most known for. Other theories include "Edda" as a corruption of Oddi, Snorri's hometown. Somewhat confusingly, the Prose Edda contains quite a bit of poetry; the "prose" descriptor was added after Snorri revised it to include prose commentary on the poetic elements. It was also called the Younger Edda due to its drawing on older sources while adding Snorri's own touches. These include a prologue that mentions the Christian stories of the Garden of Eden and Noah's Ark. (Lin, 2017)

This was not unusual - in fact, many accounts of Norse religious practices were made by Christian writers who were writing about events that had taken place several centuries earlier. To followers of Christianity, all non-Christians were "heathens", and it is unfortunate that most of our written records of ancient Nordic religions come to us from writers who were likely to have been judging the beliefs of these so-called heathens. This has led some scholars to speculate that many Norse stories as they came to use were overly influenced by the Christianization of Scandinavia, or perhaps even complete fabrications. Other schools of thought put more credence in these early accounts, and many scholars strive to split the difference, looking to use these texts as a path to enlightenment about early Norse practices, without assuming that they give a complete or totally accurate picture. (Näsström, 1999)

There is also a second famous Edda known as the Poetic Edda. The Poetic Edda was discovered in the 17th century by a bishop who collected Norse literature. It contained many similarities to Snorri's Edda, and was called the Poetic Edda because, rather simply, unlike Snorri's it contained no prose. It was also called the Elder Edda because it was believed to be the older of the two texts. Historians believe that the Elder Edda was compiled around 1270 CE. It has never been determined who compiled it. (Lin, 2017) The Poetic Edda is another major source of our knowledge about the Norse gods and goddesses, and it also contains stories of other ancient Norse heroes and the enemies they fought against. (Wigington, 2018)

In addition to the Eddas, there are also some mentions of Scandinavian culture in Arabic sources, stories passed along from those who had traveled to Scandinavia. The most famous of these is Ahmad Ihn Fadlan, whose writing we'll get to a bit later. Outside these sources, the best information we have is from archeology, such as jewelry bearing symbols or likenesses of the Norse gods (NMD, n.d.e), and from literature. Besides the Eddas, we can also learn about Norse and Viking society through early Scandinavian literature called sagas. The sagas were epic stories that usually centered around a few main characters and all of their exploits.

Perhaps the most famous of the sagas is the Volsunga Saga, about a family of heroes (the Volsung family, which is where the saga gets its name). The most famous Volsunga characters are a dragonslayer named Sigurd and a Viking shield maiden named Brynnhildr. You may recognize versions of these from more modern culture, like Wagner's famous "ring cycle" operas. Two other well-known sagas are the Laxdaela Saga and the Orkneyinga Saga. The Laxdaela Saga is about a woman named Guðrún Ósvífursdóttir and a man named Keltill Flatnose (truly); it is about the love triangle these characters get involved in, as well as a number of other common saga themes like battles and fate. The Orkneyinga Saga is - you might have guessed - about the history of the Orkney Islands. (Wigington, 2018)

Because these are literary rather than non-fiction accounts, we cannot look to them for factual information about daily life. However, they can tell us something about what the medieval Norse people believed, including what they valued and how they thought about the world around them. And for our purposes, this is the most important part. We want to know the roots of the worldview that we're embracing when we choose to practice Norse magic.

FROM AESIR TO RAGNAROK - EARLY NORSE RELIGION

The most powerful Norse gods such as Thor and Odin were known as "aesir", a word which was likely derived from one of two roots - "ansaz", which is a pillar or pole, or "ansuz", which means "life." Either of these origins suggests that the gods were seen as an intrinsic part of the world. They were also called "regin", which meant ruler. (McCoy, n.d.f) So despite not having direct Norse sources about their religious practices, we can see from their language where they placed their gods in the hierarchy of existence.

Nordic people believed their gods were everywhere - in their airy home in Asgard, but in the natural world as well.

I do want to take a moment to distinguish the early Norse beliefs from pantheistic ideas of divinity and nature. Pantheism is the belief that all parts of the world are divine, that every element of life is connected to and part of an all-encompassing divinity. (Reese, 2000) Rather than this, the Norse gods were believed to manifest in the natural world - for example, Thor was in the thunder, and his wife Sif was in the grain of the fields. (McCoy, n.d.f)

Another example of this sort of thinking can be seen through the existence of land spirits, known as landvættir. Unlike the major gods of the pantheon, these spirits were local beings who were believed to have inhabited the country even before humans. Sacrificing to the landvættir was a common practice; their favor could protect you or bring you luck, especially in endeavors related to the land such as hunting or farming. (Short, n.d.) So for Norse pagans in the middle ages, you might worship several of the larger gods that you shared with the rest of Norse society, and you also would have what were basically neighborhood gods who could influence smaller matters.

Another idea prominent in Norse religion was the respect for the warrior. We know Norse and Viking culture valued warrior skills and fighting ability highly because there was a special place in Asgard (where the gods lived, remember) for warriors who died in battle. This place was called Valhalla, and it was a fighter's paradise - a place where they could train endlessly and never die; where their injuries healed themselves; and where they were given feasts every night. This treatment was not just a reward, however. All the warriors who went to Valhalla were meant to rise up and fight on behalf of the gods when the end of the world came. (Wilkes, 2021)

The last belief I want to mention here is the concept of fate. Fate was a crucial element of Norse beliefs, and nobody - not even the gods - could change the fate that was allotted to them. In fact, Norse mythology - which we'll discuss further in the next chapter -

has one of the most famous and extreme examples of fate in the form of Ragnarök, which was a predetermined final battle that would end the world. (McCoy, n.d.f) It was believed Ragnarök would be heralded by cataclysmic events like the sun going out, the stars disappearing, and the ocean rising to cover the land. (Wilkes, 2021) This may sound terrifying to us, but unlike some conceptions of end times, Ragnarök was not meant to be a time of punishment or moral redress. Rather, the Norse just accepted that, as all things had a beginning, they also had an end. And true to form, the Norse believed the end would come in the form of an epic battle.

WHAT'S A BLÓT?

There's more to a religion than its abstract tenets. Rituals are a huge part of any religion, and early Norse paganism was no different. Like many other pagan religions, such as the Celts, the Greeks, and the Romans, the Norse people believed in offering sacrifices to the gods in order to gain divine favor. In the Nordic language, these sacrificial rituals were called "blóts.. Snorri Sturluson provided the details of a major blót in another of his epic poems, the Saga of Hakon the Good. According to Snorri, everyone would gather at the temple where the sacrifice was performed, and afterward the meat from the sacrifice would be cooked and eaten. During the feast, toasts would be made to deities, to fallen kin, and to future honor in battle. (NMD, n.d.i)

The point of ritual sacrifices and other blóts was to appease the gods so they would give you their favor. Being in a god's favor meant that good things would happen in your life. Your crops would grow well, your children would be many, your boats would sail well and carry you to far lands where you would be victorious in all your battles and reap bountiful plunder. Unlike the Christian god, for example, who demanded sacrifices as recompense for sins committed, the Norse gods simply liked sacrifices and were more inclined to help those who appeased this desire.

Author Daniel McCoy draws a comparison between the god-human relationship and the chieftain-warrior relationship, pointing out that warriors who were loyal and fought well would be given a share of the chieftain's wealth. He then points out that as Christian ideas became more prevalent in Norse society, bringing with them the idea of one God who demanded fealty on moral grounds rather than reciprocal arrangements, the relationship between chieftains and their warrior also became based on unwavering loyalty as a point of honor, rather than a mutually beneficial exchange. (McCoy, n.d.f)

Other sagas and literature give us more clues as to how rituals were performed and who was involved. Officials called magnates were often in charge of ritual sacrifices as well as the celebration of festivals and other holy days. These magnates were responsible for the organization of the blót, including hosting if the gathering was large enough, and providing food and drink. They would also perform the rituals, acting as "Godar" (priests). (NMD, n.d.i)

The Godar most likely made sacrifices at large ceremonies, but it was possible that any individual could make smaller sacrifices to their chosen deities, or in honor of their ancestors or fallen kin. In addition to the Godar, there were also women called "völur" who were believed to be able to make prophecies and divine the future. (Wilkes, 2021)

There are written records of Norse people, especially the Vikings, offering humans as sacrifices in addition to animals. There's been a lot of discussion over the accuracy of these records, which were similar to the Eddas and sagas - secondhand accounts written after the fact. This is a matter upon which we have no satisfactory answers. There have been some archeological finds that seem to suggest human sacrifice - specifically, skeletons have been found in ancient wells, suggesting that bodies had been thrown into the wells as offerings to Odin, to whom wells were sacred.

(NMD, n.d.b) Archeological finds are always a matter of interpretation, and so the question of whether or not the Norse made human sacrifices, and if so, how common it was, remains open for discussion.

TREES AND TEMPLES - HOW THE NORSE WORSHIPED

In contrast, one aspect of Norse religious rites that is generally agreed upon is that rituals were rarely practiced indoors. Instead, the ancient Norse pagans believed that certain natural features were holy - places like oak groves or bodies of water. As mentioned above, sometimes wells, though manmade, were also considered sacred through their association with water and with the god Odin. (Wilkes, 2021) The lack of systemic organization also possibly contributed to this practice, as little religious oversight meant Norse pagans could practice their religion wherever and whenever they chose.

Trees in particular were often seen as sacred to the ancient Norse people, and large trees were not only sacred sites but believed to bestow good luck and protect you from harm. The most famous tree in Norse legend was Yggdrasil, the world tree. There was also a legend of a tree at Uppsala in Sweden that stayed green even in the middle of winter. In addition to trees and bodies of water, man-made items like earthen mounds and standing stones might also be places of worship. Common religious tools, according to poems and sagas, would be armrings for swearing oaths and bowls for collecting the blood of sacrificial animals. (Short, n.d.)

One caveat to this fact is that there is a small amount of archeological evidence suggesting that, especially in the later years of paganism, some religious rites were practiced in wooden temples. This type of larger religious building is often thought to be indicative of the stratification of Norse society into a greater number of social classes (richer families might build such a temple as a sign of status) as well as part of a growing influence of southern European cultures, which had already converted to Christianity. Despite the Christian influence, however, temples like this were often destroyed in later centuries. (Metcalfe, 2020)

Temples are also occasionally described in poetry and other texts (Short, n.d.), and one major archeological discovery in recent years was a wooden temple that's estimated to have been built in the 700s CE. The first of its kind to be found in Norway, the temple was discovered in a small village on Norway's western coast. This temple is what would be called a "god house", a place of worship for events with a larger attendance than small family rituals or more simple outdoor ceremonies. Archeologists guess that holy day celebrations, such as the summer and winter solstices, would have happened in buildings like this. There would be wooden sculptures that represented the gods - the food and alcohol of the celebrations would be offered first to the gods, and then consumed by the gathered crowd. (Metcalfe, 2020)

NORSE RITUALS: SHIP BURIALS AND WALKING UNDER THE EARTH

Another major archeological find was also discovered in Norway, one that tells us something about medieval Norse burial practices. A well-preserved longship was buried in a grave, and it was filled with many wealthy possessions, as well as the remains of a pair of women and some horses. All of this is indicative of the grave owner's significance. They were most likely a royal or part of the noble class - it was common for important people to be given a ship burial, either through actual burying of the body and ship, or through pushing the ship out into the sea and then setting it on fire. (Wilkes, 2021)

Ahmad Ibn Fadlan, who I mentioned briefly earlier, also offers some insight into Norse funeral practices. An Arab writer who traveled to Scandinavia in the tenth century, Ibn Fadlan suppos-

edly attended a Viking funeral himself. According to him, the ceremony involved brutal practices such as torture and human
sacrifice. (Wilkes, 2021) It is impossible to know with certainty
that Ibn Fadlan understood everything he observed, or that he
reported it faithfully - but the discovery of the women's bodies in
the longship burial does seem to support his claims of human
sacrifice.

Ahmad Ibn Fadlan also joined a group of voyagers who were
visiting the Bulghars in 921. They sailed up the Volga River and
Ibn Fadlan recorded his interactions with the Norse tradesmen
they met there. According to Ibn Fadlan, the first thing that the
Norsemen did when they arrived was go to a carved wooden idol
that was placed in the ground near the docks. They offered the idol
food and alcohol, exhorting the gods it represented to give them
good fortune in their trading endeavors. Ibn Fadlan specifically
mentions that the tradesmen prostrated themselves before the idol,
a practice that is mentioned in other accounts of Norse religious
practices as well. (Short, n.d.)

Most of the rituals we've discussed so far have been rather serious, dealing with death and sacrifice. But not every Norse ritual is
so grim in tone. One of my favorite rituals from ancient Norse
culture is something called the "ganga undir jarðarmen." "Ganga
undir jarðarmen" literally means "to walk under the adornment of
the Earth", and this ritual was performed by removing turf from
the ground in strips which were then suspended in the air via
spears, making a kind of arbor that could be walked under. This
ceremony is mentioned in several epics, many of which offer
different reasons for performing it - for swearing fealty, for atone-
ment or absolution, and even for healing. Which of these was the
original purpose of the ritual is unknown, but it seems clear that it
was used as an element of transformation, as participants would
pass under in one state and emerge in another. (Näsström, 1999)

I really love the idea of symbolically passing "under" the earth
in order to mark your transition to a new chapter in your life, or

your commitment to a new relationship. And while it's unlikely you or I are going to dig up turf and hang it from spears in order to perform this ritual, the idea behind the "ganga undir jarðarmen" can easily be adapted using a modern-day arbor or some other symbolic passageway. The early Norse people saw sacred spaces in the world around them, and we can, as well. I really appreciate that we can be inspired by ancient ceremonies whose concepts still feel applicable in modern life.

WHEN CHRISTIANITY TOOK OVER (OR DID IT?)

Christianity took the longest to reach the northernmost parts of Europe, so the areas that became modern-day Sweden, Norway, and Iceland were the last strongholds of earlier pagan beliefs. While Christian writers are responsible for much of what we know about the pagan world of pre-Christian Scandinavia, the coming of Christianity was also responsible for large parts of the culture being destroyed or going underground. Each of these countries navigated the transition from paganism to Christianity differently, meaning in some places old traditions were kept alive or merged with Christianity, while in other places those traditions were lost forever.

Norway was conquered by an invading Christian king (Olaf I), who started the country's conversion. King Olaf II continued in his footsteps, both using force rather than persuasion to convert their subjects. Iceland, on the other hand, was converted by vote of parliament, but with an understanding that many pagan practices could still be practiced privately. This contrast meant that Iceland preserved many pagan practices which disappeared in Norway. Sweden, meanwhile, was the last of the countries to convert to Christianity. Historians don't know much about Sweden's conversion, but it appears that the population was quite resistant, often driving out would-be Christian kings. (Turville-Petre & Polomé, 2006)

It's important to realize that while Christianity eventually overtook paganism as the dominant religion in all three countries, it was rarely a cut and dried process. There were compromises, such as Iceland's parliament allowing pagans to keep their faith so long as they didn't practice it in public. The Vikings were also known to "adopt" Christianity for the purposes of trade relations. These Vikings would have a cross inscribed on them - called a "primsigning" - as a concession to Christians who otherwise would not trade with the Vikings. Often the first major conversions of political leaders happened for similar reasons, to facilitate international relations. Many of the Norse people were not bothered by adding the Christian god to the other gods they worshiped. Some archeological finds illustrate this overlap of beliefs, such as coins found in England which bear the symbol of Mjölnir as well as the name of St. Peter. (Wilkes, 2021)

This mingling of the old and new brings us back to our discussion at the beginning of the chapter, that early Norse society was rarely a monolith where everyone held the exact same beliefs and practiced them in exactly the same way. This is something to keep in mind in your own practice, as well. You don't have to do things the way anyone else does them. The old Norse beliefs were a collection of ideas and gods, from which individuals could choose those things that resonated with them. There were shared commonalities, but there was also room for variation, and even the occasional foreign god.

In the next chapter, we'll dive a bit deeper into Norse mythology - it's time to meet the gods and monsters that roamed (and still do roam) the Norse imagination.

CHAPTER 2

NINE REALMS, BOUND BY A TREE

I n the beginning, there was a void. Into that void came a freezing mist and a burning fire, and together they made... a giant cow. Yes, you read that correctly - Norse mythology starts with the creation of a magical cow. (Knightly, n.d.a) That probably sounds a bit strange, but if you examine creation mythology from all over the world, most of it sounds a bit strange. You might not have heard of Auðumbla (the cow), but you've probably heard of the other being that was born from the marriage of fire and ice - a giant. The giant's name was Ymir.

The creation of these two beings is the first step in a complex story that I won't get into at the moment - though it is very interesting if you're into mythology (if so, I encourage you to read up about it!) I want to fast forward a few generations, though, until we get to the birth of Odin and his two brothers. The three of them were the sons of the first god (Buri) and a giantess, and together they killed Ymir, and turned him into the world, with his body becoming the land and his blood becoming the seas. (Scott, 2021)

So the world was made in violence and bloodshed, which is not surprising given what we know of the Norse and their valorization of strength and the ability to fight. And the world was made through division, as Odin and his brothers forced the cold from the void (Niflheim) under the earth, and then divided their own world, Midgard, from Jötunheim, where the jötunar (creatures sometimes known as giants) lived. But the world was also made in creation, as they took flames from the fiery part of the void (Muspelheim) into the stars, and then made the first two humans, Ask and Embla, from an ash tree and an elm tree. (Knightly, n.d.a)

I started this chapter with the creation myth because I believe it illustrates so much of the characteristics of the Norse religion that we've already discussed. The gods are shown to be powerful and connected to the natural world; there is a necessary sacrifice that results in the bountiful giving of life; and of course, there are trees and giants. As we look more deeply at the mythology that the ancient Norse people used to explain the world, remember that the point of this mythology is not factual history, but meaningful stories - stories that both shaped and were shaped by the people that told them.

THE NINE REALMS

Norse mythology believed there were more worlds than just our own - specifically, they believed in nine different realms, although these nine realms are never listed. Many have speculated about these realms and made their own lists. Generally, though, you can assume that our world (Midgard) was one of the realms, as well as Asgard and Vanaheim, realms of the gods. (The realms of Asgard and Midgard have a special link, a rainbow bridge called the Bifrost.) Jötunheim is usually included, as are Niflheim, the ice realm, and Muspelheim, the fire realm. Other common entries include the realms of the elves (Alfheim), the dwarves (Svartalfheim), and the dead (Hel) - although according to some, Niflheim is the realm of the dead. (McCoy, n.d.a)

While the Bifrost connected Asgard and Midgard, there was

something else that connected all of these realms. I've actually already mentioned it - it's the world tree Yggdrasil. Yggdrasil was an ash tree, one of the most sacred kinds of trees. It was believed this tree grew at the heart of all existence, and that all the realms were connected to one another through its roots and branches. (Wilkes, 2021) All kinds of creatures live in or on Yggdrasil, including a dragon in its roots, an eagle in its top branches, and a squirrel that travels the whole tree carrying messages. (Knightly, n.d.p) In addition to all these creatures, the world tree was also one of the places the gods would regularly gather.

My favorite thing about Yggdrasil is that its roots also hold three magical wells. These wells were called Hvergelmir, Mímis-brunnr, and Urðarbrunnr. Mímisbrunnr belonged to Mímir, a wise water god; it was here that Odin gave up one of his eyes in order to drink from the well and gain great knowledge. The other two wells, Hvergelmir and Urðarbrunnr, were balancing forces. Hvergelmir was where the dragon lived, and it was constantly chewing on Yggdrasil's roots and causing it to wither. However, the water from Urðarbrunnr had revitalizing powers, and would bring the tree back to life. (Britannica, 1998) In this way, Yggdrasil and its wells represented the cyclical nature of life, death, and rebirth.

THE MANY GODS OF ASGARD AND BEYOND

By now you've probably figured out that Norse religion was a polytheistic one - "poly" meaning "many" and "theistic" referencing gods. The fact that early Norse peoples had many gods made them similar to other ancient religions and in opposition to (relatively) newer, monotheistic religions with only one god, like Christianity, Judaism, and Islam. Often these gods would be known by similar but slightly different names in different regions. (Näsström, 1999)

Just like the days of the week, there are many places in modern-day Scandinavia where the names were inspired by the names of the Norse gods. Parsing out these names can indicate which god was worshiped in a region. For example, the name of the city of Odense, Denmark evolved from a combination of "Odin's" with the word "vi" or "ve." (NMD, n.d.i) The suffix "vé" in the name of a location designated that place as a consecrated place. (Short, n.d.) We can therefore guess that centuries before it was a thriving modern metropolis, Odense was a place where sacrifices were made to Odin.

Most of the Norse gods were believed to live in Asgard, which hovered far above earth (remember, it took a special magical bridge to reach Asgard from earth). The gods often fought with their sworn enemies, the giants, who lived outside Asgard on the margins of the world. Other enemies of the gods came in the form of giant creatures, such as a supernaturally strong wolf called Fenrir and a serpent living in the sea that encircled the whole world. (NMD, n.d.e)

I say "most" of the Norse gods lived in Asgard because the gods and goddesses of Norse mythology were actually divided into two different types - the Aesir and the Vanir. This is why there are actually two different realms for the gods listed among the nine realms. The Aesir live in Asgard and the Vanir live in Vanaheim. Most of the gods you will hear about in Norse myths are Aesir. The Aesir were believed to control the universe and keep things running smoothly. Odin, Thor, Baldur, Frigg, Heimdall, and Tyr were all Aesir. (McCoy, n.d.b)

However, there were three gods from the Vanir that made frequent appearances - Njord and his children, Freyr and Freyja. The reason for this is probably because, despite being of the Vanir, they lived in Asgard. Though they were all gods, the Aesir and the Vanir did not always get along. After one of their wars, an uneasy peace was established. In order to maintain that peace, it was decided that Njord, Freyr, and Freyja would go to live among the Aesir in Asgard. (Scott, 2021)

Below is some more detailed information about the most important gods - Odin, Thor, Loki, Freyja, and Freyr - as well as quick descriptions for a few other personal favorites of mine - Baldur, Heimdall, Frigga, and Tyr.

ODIN

Odin ruled Asgard, and he was known as the "all-father." He valued wisdom above all else, to the point where he endured physical trials and disfigurement in order to gain that knowledge. In addition to giving up his eye so he could drink from Mímir's well, he also hung on a great ash tree for nine days and nine nights in order to understand the mysteries of the runes. (Wilkes, 2021) It's very likely that this tree was the world tree, Yggsdrasil. (Knightly, n.d.p)

As the all-father, Odin was something of a patriarch of the Norse pantheon, and he was especially popular among men in positions of power. (NMD, n.d.a) Sometimes he rode a giant horse with eight legs called Sleipnir, but he also liked to wander the world in disguise (usually as an old man in a wide-brimmed hat and cloak. He was associated with ravens and was said to have two ravens in particular, named Hugin and Munin, that traveled the world and reported their findings back to him. (Wilkes, 2021)

Thor

Thor was beloved because he was uncomplicated and trustworthy, which also meant he was associated with the rule of law and keeping order. (NMD, n.d.a) He was seen as a protector, tasked with guarding both humanity and the gods. He was a warrior, strong enough to go toe to toe with the giants. His weapon of choice, his hammer Mjölnir, is probably almost as well known as he is.

Thor was famously associated with stormy weather, and in particular with lightning and thunder. (Wilkes, 2021) Because of this association, he was also sometimes thought to control the rain.

In times of drought, Thor might be offered a sacrifice as a supplication that he would send rain. (Wigington, 2019) In some versions of Norse mythology, thunder and lightning are not just associated with Thor but are actually made by him, a product of his journeys through the sky in his goat-drawn chariot.

LOKI

By virtue of his prominence in the Marvel movies and comics, Loki is probably the best-known Norse god besides Thor and Odin. Sometimes Loki is cast as the villain of tales, and he certainly was responsible for his fair share of wrongdoing. However, his main trait was not evil but trickery. He was not always bad, but he was never to be trusted. Mirroring this, he possessed the ability to shapeshift, being able to change into anyone or anything. (Wilkes, 2021) Interestingly, unlike the other gods, Loki is not believed to have had followers. (Wigington, 2019)

Loki is something of a hybrid god, as he was originally from Jötunheim but he and Odin have a blood bond, which gave him standing among the Asgardians. You could say that Loki's weakness is that he is untrustworthy, but the gods' weakness is that they cannot resist trying to use his skills of deception to their advantage. In fact, Thor's hammer and quite a few other beloved treasures of the gods were only created because Loki tricked the dwarves into making them. (NMD, n.d.a)

FREYJA

Goddesses weren't nearly as common as gods in the Norse pantheon, but the goddess Freyja was both powerful and beloved. Similarly to Venus in the Roman tradition and Aphrodite in the Greek tradition, Freyja was a goddess of love and beauty. Unlike those two, she was also the goddess of magic. She also owned a cloak that gave her the ability to fly. Like Odin's Valhalla, Freyja also had a cohort of fallen warriors who she trained for the final battle in a field called Fólkvangr. (Wilkes, 2021)

Freyja was also associated with prophecy and the practice of seidr, a female-dominated magical art (more about this later in the book!). (NMD, n.d.a) And she was associated with fertility, childbirth, and marriage. Perhaps the strangest (and possibly my favorite) of Freyja's attributes is that she was said to weep not water, but gold. (Wigington, 2019)

FREYR

Freyr, sometimes spelled Frey, was Freyja's brother. He and Freyja were the children of Njord, god of the sea. Freyr was a sun god who could bless his worshippers with prosperity. He was given offerings in exchange for fruitfulness, both for crops and children. He had many magical items, such as a ship that could be kept in his pocket and a sword that fought by itself. Freyr rode a boar instead of a horse. The boar was made for him from gold by the dwarves (Wilkes, 2021) (As you can probably tell by now, many of the magical items owned by the gods were made by the dwarves). The boar was called Gullinborsti, and it was supposedly faster than any horse, no matter whether Freyr rode him over land or sea. (NMD, n.d.a)

BALDUR

Baldur was a god of light, and always described as beautiful to behold. He was tragically killed by a trick of Loki's, something which backfired quite badly for Loki. This is because Baldur was so well-loved by his fellow gods - in fact, he might have been the most well-loved of all the gods. (Wigington, 2019) Though the story of Baldur might be a tragic one, I like it because it has a shred of hope - supposedly after Ragnörak, a new world will be born, and Baldur will be reborn with it.

HEIMDALL

Heimdall was another god of light, and he is also a protector to the gods and their realm. Because of this, Heimdall is always positioned on the Bifrost, keeping enemies out and ready to sound the alarm on his horn. (Wigington, 2019) Heimdall is the embodiment of loyalty and vigilance, and I like him because he uses his strength and his extraordinary senses to protect his home and the others who live there.

FRIGGA

Frigga was married to Odin. She was also associated with seeing the future, sometimes by way of weaving it - though she had no control over the fates she wove. There are not a lot of stories about Frigga, but sometimes she is said to be responsible for the creation of runes. (Wigington, 2019) I think it's really interesting that Odin was said to have to hang without food or water for nine days in order to understand the runes, but it's possible that his wife was wise and powerful enough to be the one that created them.

TYR

Tyr is a warrior god, patron of victors. He was a particularly brave god, which won him many admirers but also lost him his hand. The story goes that he was so brave he put his hand in the mouth of the great wolf Fenrir - but the wolf betrayed him and bit it off. (Wigington, 2019) To me, Tyr personifies the Norse ideal of fearlessness - and the fact that you might lose a hand, but you'll get an incredible story out of it.

OTHER BEINGS

Perhaps the most well-known beings in Norse mythology outside of the gods were the giants. We already learned about Ymir, the first giant or Jötunn (Jötunn is the singular, Jötnar is the plural). Other well-known Jötnar are Hel, who was in charge of the underworld, and Fenrir, who was a giant wolf foretold to kill Odin at the end of the world.

One last note about the giants. I noted earlier that "giants" is the most frequent translation for "Jötnar" - the two terms are used rather interchangeably. But a more accurate translation of the name would be "devourers", as they were known not so much for their size as for the disorder and darkness they wrought. (McCoy, n.d.b) In this way, the Jötnar were natural enemies of the gods, who were tasked with keeping the universe ordered.

Other important creatures in Norse mythology include the elves, the valkyries, and the norns. There were two tribes of elves, the light elves and the dark elves. Because the dark elves live in Svartalfheim, the same realm as the dwarves, it's been suggested that dark elves might actually be another term for the dwarves. (Scott, 2021) The valkyries worked for Odin; it was them that guided slain warriors to Valhalla. (McCoy, n.d.a) The valkyries were also said to have sway over which side triumphed on the battlefield. (McCoy, n.d.b)

And last, but certainly not least, the norns. The norns are maybe my favorite characters in all of Norse mythology. Sometimes called the fates, the norns lived at the base of the Yggdrasil and were in charge of weaving the lives of both the humans and the gods. (NMD, n.d.e) It's the norns who give the water from Urðarbrunnr its magical ability to keep the world tree alive. (Knightly, n.d.p) And unlike Frigga, the norns could actually change your fate - but once they had set your fate, no one else had the power to change it. Remember that fate is a crucial part of the

Norse belief system, and therefore the norns held a very important position in Norse mythology.

Now that you've got a solid understanding of historic Norse religious beliefs and the stories that underpinned them, we can take a look at modern Norse paganism. On to the next chapter!

CHAPTER 3

THE NEW OLD WAYS

T he Hjaltadalur valley in the northern part of Iceland might not seem to have much in common with the market town of Newark in the United Kingdom, but the two places have an unlikely connection - both are locations for temples created by modern-day practitioners of Norse religions. The temple in Newark is housed in a restored chapel, where members of the local Odinist Fellowship meet. The Newark Odinists employ a Cup of Remembrance and readings from the Eddas in their worship; their temple's only decoration is portraits of the Norse gods that the Fellowship commissioned for the space. (Parker, 2015) The temple in Iceland was built from scratch, stone and turf filling out a wooden frame, by a local farmer. It is where the local chapter of Ásatrúarfélagið, an Icelandic religious organization that grew out of a revived version of Iceland's ancient Norse religion, meet to celebrate major feasts as well as for informal meetings meant to foster community. (Helgason, 2015)

The two temples are home to two different versions of modern Norse religion based on ancient Norse practices - Odinism and Ásatrúarfélagið. One is a repurposed structure that once belonged to another religion, the other is a new structure. The methods and end goals of their congregants' worship are not necessarily the same. Two things do unequivocally link the temples, however. Worshippers at both are inspired by Norse traditions, and religious leaders for both emphasize that anyone - regardless of religious affiliation - is welcome to join. (Parker, 2015; Helgason, 2015)

While the rest of this chapter is devoted to an in-depth look at modern Norse religion, its history and current state, I've just covered two of the most important things to know: all of these traditions are in some way inspired by what we know of the early Scandinavian world, and the religion is a very open one - you do not need to profess any specific belief or follow any specific tenets to participate. This combination of tradition and flexibility makes modern Norse religion quite unique, and adaptable to each individual's religious needs.

HOW HEATHENRY HAS MODERNIZED

You already know about the early Norse civilizations and the way Christianity eventually became the dominant religion in Scandinavia. In the 20th century, a number of older pagan religions have not only resurfaced but grown quite a bit in popularity. The term "heathenry" is sometimes used as an umbrella term for the modern pagan traditions that are related to Norse history (though it can also refer to other practices from the pre-Christian time period in northern Europe, that are not Norse in origin). Many of the key beliefs of these religions have already been introduced through our discussions of history and mythology in the previous chapters. The main deities, for example, are usually the Aesir, the Vanir, and the Jötnar. These deities and other magical forces are believed to be part of everyday life (animism), ancestors are often venerated alongside deities, and fate plays a large role. (Time Nomads, 2021)

One thing that has changed from medieval practices in most cases is the types of sacrifices that are offered. Many modern Norse pagans choose to "sacrifice" objects (this is known as an artifact offering) rather than animals (and of course, no matter the historical debate on the subject, no modern practitioners are making human sacrifices). There is some evidence that suggests artifact sacrifices were also part of ancient practices, most commonly by leaving a precious object in a bog or body of water. (Time Nomads, 2021)

While there are a variety of ways that heathenry is practiced, there are two broad categories into which we can sort these ways: whether the aim is to get as close to the old Norse ways as you can, which is called "Reconstructionism", or to reinvent the old ways in practices that reflect present-day values and beliefs, which is called "Revivalism." (Knightly, n.d.k) Because the terms are so similar, I found it hard to remember which was which at first. My trick is to remind myself that a revival is the second time something has been alive, and therefore Revivalism is a second or modern version of Norse religion. In contrast, a reconstruction is rebuilding of the same thing again, so Reconstructionists are trying to rebuild the original religion.

Other differences in religious beliefs and conduct will be found between cultures, between communities, and even between families. (Knightly, n.d.k) This is because, again, there is no central authority and no foundational scripture for Norse paganism. Other religions that rely heavily on hierarchical structure, behavioral mores, and adherence to scriptural dogma are known as "high demand" religions, while Norse paganism lacks these and is known as a "decentralized" religion. (Knightly, n.d.g) Within this decentralized format, there are some groups that have chosen to form more structured organizations, while others stick with looser groupings based on existing social structures such as families or friend circles. (BBC, 2003)

One thing to be careful of is the Völkisch roots of some forms of heathenry. Around the time that Naziism was taking hold in Germany, many white supremacist thinkers were looking to old Germanic cultures for so-called "pure" traditions and beliefs.

Many of these ideas started well before the rise of the Nazi party, in the wave of German Romanticism that pushed back against Enlightenment ideas of form and order and sought to reconnect with nature and the expression of intense emotions. However, some German Romantics began gatekeeping the German identity, creating the Völk movement which claimed to represent the true Germany, but in fact was based on exclusion and antisemitic sentiment. There are strains of Odinism and Ásatrú that are still associated with white supremacist groups even today. (Knightly, n.d.f) These strains could be especially strong in early Reconstructionism because of the emphasis on historical "accuracy" (though this accuracy was often muddied by biased readings of history). However, these groups failed in their recreations, often because they were more interested in the appearance of the religion than in its doctrine. (Knightly, n.d.k)

ÁSATRÚ AND THE RETURN OF THE OLD GODS

Perhaps the most well-known denomination of modern Norse paganism is Ásatrú. Practitioners of Ásatrú center their religion around the Aesir. The literal translation of Ásatrú is "true to the Aesir." This name, and the names of other forms of Norse paganism, are inspired by the gods and other beings in Norse mythology. I want to note, however, that these are not names that were used in medieval Norse society. The pagan religions were merely called "forn sidr", which means "the old way", which distinguished those religious practices from the newer Christian ones. (NMD, n.d.d)

Ásatrú loosely maintains the traditional structure of the religion in medieval times, with a high priest over the whole religion, and local priests ("Goði") for each congregation or region (a "goðorð"). (Staff IM, 2019) Individual priests are called "Gode" and "Gydje", depending on their gender. (NMD, n.d.d) It focuses on the Hávamál, a portion of the Poetic Edda, as a guide for religious practice. The terminology used by practitioners, such as "folk" for the congregations and "kindred" for the larger groups or chapters, reflects the communal emphasis of Ásatrú. (Time Nomads, 2021)

Ásatrú is most strongly associated with Iceland, where it has been an official, state-recognized religion since 1973. (Remember, Iceland had officially demoted its pagan religion in 1000 CE, when its parliament voted to make Christianity the only official religion of Iceland.) The official status came at the request of citizens who were practicing the religion, and in addition to official religious status, Iceland also has Ásatrúarfélagið, Ásatrú's official organization, which was founded in 1992. Ásatrúarfélagið has specifically decried the white nationalist influence of some other branches of Ásatrú and other heathenry, and the association with the aggressive and bloody elements of Norse, and particularly Viking, history. Instead, the organization values the ideas of respect and harmonious living among all people. (Staff IM, 2019)

Ásatrú is the fastest-growing religious denomination in Iceland and it has the most adherents outside of the Christian faiths. (Staff IM, 2019) And while the Icelandic version of Ásatrú is perhaps the most well-known, the religion was gaining popularity in many other places at around the same time, including in the United States, where groups like the Ásatrú Folk Assembly and the Ásatrú Alliance were formed. (Wigington, 2019b)

Denmark also has its own version of Ásatrú, albeit with some marked differences. First, in Denmark the term Ásatrú is not often used. When it is used, it is often spelled "asatro." However, the officially recognized Norse pagan association is actually called Forn Sidr, as a nod to the practice's roots. And while Icelandic pagans have started to build temples - such as the one mentioned at the beginning of this chapter - in which to hold their ceremonies, it is still most common for Danish pagans to hold their ceremonies outside, preferably in a place that has connections to the pre-Christian medieval Norse society. (NMD, n.d.d)

Whatever it is called, the popularity of the religion around the world, and the fact that its formation and recognition has been driven organically by practitioners, is indicative of another difference with Christianity. Most Christian denominations are evangelical, meaning they encourage their followers to proselytize, actively converting others into the religion. In the heyday of Christianity's spread, this sort of conversion was aided by politics and military might. In contrast, Ásatrú - and most other Norse pagan religions - does not instruct its practitioners to seek converts. Instead, the religion has spread as people have discovered it while searching for a practice that resonates with them.

BEYOND ÁSATRÚ

I mentioned the temple in Newark at the beginning of this chapter, and you may remember that the congregants there were members of an Odinist fellowship. Sometimes the term Odinist refers to groups that grew out of German Romanticism in the middle of the twentieth century (Knightly, n.d.f), other times it refers to groups that focus on Odin more heavily than other Norse deities. There are groups that also focus on other deities - Loki is a popular one, and his adherents are called Lokeans. (Time Nomads, 2021) Other forms of heathenry or Norse paganism include The Northern Tradition and Germanic Pagan Reconstructionism. (BBC, 2003)

There are also the traditions of Vanatru and Rökkatru. Vanatru centers on the deities of the Vanir, and it is an offshoot of Ásatrú (you might have guessed the translation of its name: "true to the Vanir"). However, Vanatru is usually less communal and less organized than Ásatrú. There is often more variety in deity veneration for Vanatru, and because the Vanir are often associated with nature and magic, followers of Vanatru are more likely to practice magic and engage in nature worship. Rökkatru focuses on the Jötnar and other dark or chaotic deities or beings, and puts even more emphasis on the individual than Vanatru, and bears many similarities to Norse shamanism. It's important to note that just because the Jötnar are described as dark, this does not mean they are considered evil. Unlike religions such as Christianity, light and dark have no morality associated with them in Norse traditions. (Time Nomads, 2021)

By now, you hopefully feel like you've got a good grasp of Norse paganism, from its origins all the way up through to the present day. (Pat yourself on the back! You learned a lot in the last three chapters.) At this point, you might have a few inklings about which parts of the religion appeal to you. But you might be wondering - how does magic fit into all this? Great question! The answers are in the next chapter, so read on.

CHAPTER 4
PRACTICAL MAGIC

"There's no such thing as magic." You've probably heard that before, right? If not in your own life, on a television show or film, usually uttered by the main character, usually right before someone or something proves them absolutely wrong by performing some fantastical feat of dazzling, Oscar-worthy magic. In many ways, this sort of scene encapsulates the relationship much of the modern world has with magic - either denying its existence, or expecting some sort of wild, sparkly demonstration of power, one that you know deep down probably isn't real.

It's okay if you love movie magic - I do, too. But if you're going to actually practice magic, it's vital that we establish what magic is, and what it isn't. It isn't a trick that you learn, or a scientific equation where you put in certain ingredients and produce certain outcomes. It isn't a fantasy novel where an old man with a beard waves his staff and makes lightning crack the sky. (Although probably the most famous of those wizards, Gandalf, borrowed more than a few characteristics from Odin himself.)

So if that's what it isn't, then what is magic? It's a way to connect to the world around us, to nature and the wilderness that we're too often cut off from in modern society. It's a way of focusing our energy, and manipulating the energy we come into contact with, in order to create a life for ourselves that's more in tune with both the world around us and our own hopes, dreams, and desires. Magic is about intention and clarity of thought, which is also where the magic you perform with Norse paganism might differ from other magical practices.

While there is no one way to practice Norse paganism, there are a number of values and philosophical ideas that you'll repeatedly encounter as you go deeper into this worldview. These values and ideas affect how you see the world, which in turn will affect how you interact with the world. And any magical practice starts there, where your actions meet the world. So this chapter will lay out the common tenets of Norse paganism and then show you how those things will factor into your own magical practice.

MANY GODS, MANY PATHS

We've already established the polytheistic nature of both old and new Norse paganism - the Norse pantheon has many gods, any of whom you can worship, but none of whom demand your worship. This is a crucial element: not just that there are many gods, but that you have a choice in which gods will become your personal gods. Unlike monotheistic religions that insist upon one true god, Norse paganism allows room for you to determine your own path. In addition to polytheism, this is also part of the idea of pluralism.

Pluralism is a philosophical concept that has to do with one's views on the nature of the world and the way that meaning and morality are categorized. Many of us are most familiar with a dualistic view of the world, in which things are described as one of two options - frequently good or bad, though it can also be masculine or feminine, divine or earthly, etc. (Knightly, n.d.g) Pluralism eschews that idea in favor of a more open approach. A pluralistic religion allows for multiple options, and for more than one thing to be true at once.

The concept of pluralism is indicative of how Norse paganism approaches morality as a whole. There is no objective, unchanging idea on what is "right" and what is "wrong." Morality isn't meant to be a set of rules that were handed down from a being on high, not to be transgressed on pain of punishment. (Knightly, n.d.h) Instead, practitioners are meant to adapt to different situations, allowing for nuance and personal interpretation.

One more quick note about polytheism in Norse paganism: There are some who believe in literal gods who, in whatever form, have independent lives and their own agency. These people believe the gods exist just as you and I do, and can interact with the world in much the same way (albeit usually with much more power). The people who believe this are known as "hard polytheists." Not everyone believes this way, however - there are also those who view the Norse gods more as ideas who exist to manifest certain traits or qualities. For these people, called "soft polytheists", the gods are reflections of the human condition, and our interactions with them are about gaining a greater understanding of the world through these "ideal" or prototypical characters. (Knightly, n.d.n)

DO THE RIGHT THING

Another major component of Norse pagan philosophy is orthopraxy. While pluralism deals with abstract ideas and the way you think about divinity and morality, orthopraxy deals with your actions. In fact, orthopraxy means "proper/correct action." (Harper, n.d.). You may be familiar with the word "orthodoxy", which has a similar root, but concerns your beliefs (the "dox" is the same as that in "doxology"). The concepts of orthodoxy and orthopraxy can stand alone or complement each other; Norse paganism emphasizes orthopraxy because it is a religion based on what we do, rather than what we believe. (Knightly, n.d.g) Just like you do not have to venerate any particular god, you do not have to adhere to any particular belief. Your actions - what you choose to do, rather than believe - are far more important.

Be careful not to fall into the trap of looking for one specific "right" thing to do, however. As we just discussed, ideas of "correctness" mean something different in pluralistic religions. So orthopraxy in practice is not about acting in accordance with certain rules; rather, it's about acting in a way that will nurture you and the world around you. I love this component of paganism, because it encourages us to assess our actions in the context of our lives, the situations we're currently in, and the larger society that we are part of. There is no "always do this" - there's only what you feel is the right course of action in the moment.

There's another idea that goes hand in hand with orthopraxy, and that's immanence. Immanence is the belief that we should enjoy our lives now, rather than living them in hopes of a promised reward in the next life. (Knightly, n.d.g) Perhaps you can see how this ties into both orthopraxy and pluralism. Because there is no eternal score sheet that will determine if you are rewarded or punished when you die, you are encouraged to find your rewards in this life, and to act with traits like kindness and compassion not because they are "good", but because they make the world a better place to live in for all of us.

THE NINE NOBLE VIRTUES (PLUS A FEW MORE)

It is common to come across the idea of the nine noble virtues, especially when you first start learning about heathenry and other forms of Norse paganism. While the religion is decentralized and pluralistic, these are some traditional virtues that were highly valued in medieval Norse society, and that many modern Norse pagans hold in high esteem. The nine noble virtues are: courage, truth, honor, fidelity, discipline, hospitality, industriousness, self-reliance, and perseverance. (Wigington, 2018b) It's important to note that not everyone connects to or otherwise uses these virtues, and that even within those who do, there can be quite a bit of variety in how the virtues are interpreted. These are not rules! They are traditions with some history that I think would be helpful for you to know and understand.

I find that they can be most helpful not as edicts, but more as touchstones. If I find myself in a difficult situation or wrestling with a hard decision, I can walk through these virtues and think about which might apply, and in what way. For example, if I am thinking about giving up on a goal I have been struggling to achieve, I might think first about whether I've followed through on the steps needed to achieve that goal (discipline), whether I've worked hard at the goal (industriousness), and whether I've stuck with the goal long enough for the fruits of my effort to appear (perseverance). If I have not achieved the goal despite all those things being true, then I might feel that I am justified in letting go of that objective and moving on to something else.

There are a few other virtues that can be found in Norse pagan thought even though they are not among the traditional nine. Some of the more common ones are wyrd, orlog, and frith. You might be familiar with wyrd if you're a fan of fantasy novels or Shakespeare, both of which feature iterations of the "wyrd sisters", three women who possess magical powers and often deal with the fate of the world. The norns are one such iteration, and if you guessed that wyrd has something to do with fate, you're correct. But wyrd is not just a vague idea of "destiny"; it is about the coming together of all things in the universe to create a "web of wyrd." (BBC, 2003) A web is the perfect way to illustrate wyrd, because it is not about a fate set in stone, but rather a future that we are all weaving together with our actions.

Because of this interwoven quality, orlog is a major part of the web of wyrd. Orlog has to do with the consequences of our actions. (Knightly, n.d.o) Orlog can be thought of in almost scientific terms, similar to Newton's third law of motion - for every action, there is an equal and opposite reaction. It can also be thought of in terms of a chain reaction, one step leading to another, and then to another; or like ripples in a pond, with the consequences of an action spreading out in all directions. However you conceptualize it, the point is to see and acknowledge the connection between what we do and what happens next.

Orlog is key in a tenet of Norse pagan faith known as "the gifting cycle." The gifting cycle encourages us to offer what we can to one another - it does not have to be a physical gift or something of great monetary value. (Knightly, n.d.e) Giving and receiving are both part of the gifting cycle, and by participating in this cycle, we help maintain balance, both personally and in the world at large. I love this principle because it frames the concepts of giving and receiving in a communal way. Giving should make us as happy as receiving, because both are part of a rhythm that helps sustain a natural equilibrium.

That equilibrium is part of another virtue, frith (also spelled fridh). You could say frith means "peace", but that is a bit of a simplistic translation. Frith is a kind of harmony that's achieved when we are healthy and happy both within ourselves and within our relationships. (Knightly, n.d.d) You as an individual should strive towards frith by taking care of your mind and body, and creating an environment that makes you happy and fulfilled. On a larger scale, a community should work toward frith by prioritizing healthy relationships and making space for everyone to thrive. Frith is perhaps my favorite virtue because it sort of encompasses all the other virtues - the point of being courageous or honest or hospitable, or any of the other virtues, is to create a life you find fulfilling and a world in which others are also free and able to find fulfillment.

FROM GALDR TO TROLLDOM - TYPES OF NORSE MAGIC

Now that you've got a good grasp on the philosophies and virtues that can help govern your use of magic, we're ready to dive into the different forms of magic that are practiced in Norse paganism. As I said in the beginning of this chapter, magic is about connecting to the world around us, focusing and manipulating energy, and harnessing the power of intention. In modern life, magic is often seen to be in opposition to science or wisdom, but for early pagan magicians, knowledge was power, including magical power. In medieval Germanic societies, to which Scandinavia belonged, practicing magic involved a great deal of wisdom. The more one understood how the world worked, the better they were able to manipulate it. (McCoy, n.d.d)

In fact, knowledge was so crucial to the early Norse understanding of knowledge that it can be found in the language itself. Scholar and author Catharina Raudvere discusses how the word "kunna" is part of the word "fjölkyngi." Fjölkyngi is a broad Norse term for magic, and kunna is related to knowledge and understanding. Fjölkyngi can be translated into "great knowledge." (McCoy, n.d.d) Therefore magic is not the abandonment of reason, observation, and common sense, but rather its application in new contexts to affect change.

Along with fjölkyngi, there are several specific types of magic, distinguished mostly by their methods or their goals, but occasionally by the type of person that commonly practiced that magic. Below I'll discuss each of these types of magic in more detail.

GALDR

Galdr has to do with words, and this ancient magical practice has had a huge influence on our modern ideas of magic - especially those that are found in our entertainment. Galdr involves incantations, what we might think of as "saying a spell." (This type of magic is also relevant to rune magic - there is much more to be said about rune magic, which we will cover in its own chapter later in the book.) Odin was also known to practice galdr, with the Hávamál relating that Odin knows at least eighteen galdr spells, which were called "galdrar." (Folmer, 2016)

You may hear about a subset of galdr called galdrastafur (or galdrastafir), which are symbols that can be carved or written in order to invoke certain protections or other simple spells. These are also called staves (the "stafur" in galdrastafur). While related to and inspired by earlier pagan practices, the actual practice of galdrastafur can only be traced back to the Renaissance. This sort of stave magic was created by pagan practitioners of that era who were drawing on the influence of earlier religions. (Folmer, 2016) The practice was influenced by mystic practices in the Judeo-Christian traditions, as well. Because it has a much more clear lineage and record, galdrastafur can be formally learned from practiced instructors. (Knightly, n.d.j)

SEIDR

We know more about seidr than we do about many other types of magic, in part because it is frequently mentioned in the Eddas and other medieval literature. Völva, the practitioners of seidr, were almost always women. (It's true that Odin was said to have practiced seidr, but he was an exception - it was historically rare for men to work this kind of magic.) The most common identifying symbol for these women was a spindle or distaff, a reference to the threads of fate in the web woven by the norns. (Vickers, 2020) From that clue, you can probably guess that the most common goals of seidr were related to divination. In fact, the word itself comes from the Old Norse word for "string" or "cord", possibly a reference to the norns with their threads of fate. (McCoy, n.d.j)

We'll get more into the divination aspects of seidr, and of other types of future-telling magic, in chapter nine. For now, just know that it is a well-known form of magic that we still don't actually know very much about. We know seidr comes from the same root word as "seeth." (Knightly, n.d.j) We know that in addition to Odin, Freyja was also believed to practice it. And there are some sources that suggest a greater purview for seidr, such as the ability not just to predict fate but to alter it, as well as power over weather or healing abilities. (Folmer, 2016) In the modern era, seidr has expanded to include things like astral projection, vision work, and trance work. (Knightly, n.d.j)

TROLLDOM

Don't let the name of this type of magic have you picturing a creature living under a bridge picking fights with goats. Trolldom, also sometimes spelled "trolldomr", is not about "trolls", specifically, and certainly not in any way modern fantasy stories might recognize. In the sense that it relates to trolldom, the term troll encompasses many different kinds of magical or otherworldly creatures. (Vickers, 2020) It is connected to nature and the land, not so much to the greater deities like the Aesir, but to local spirits who were associated with specific places.

Trolldom is folk magic, a magic of the people. It is passed from generation to generation in the same way other folk wisdom is. There can be many methods and many objectives for this magic. Like galdr, working trolldom magic often involves chanting aloud. We don't have many sources for the actual spells, but we know they were used for healing, for protection, for good luck, and for interpersonal manipulation such as causing a delay or guilting someone. Trolldom could also involve communing with ancestors or other dead souls, or predicting the future. (Knightly, n.d.j) The practice of trolldom suffered during later centuries, when the fervor of the witch hunts spread to northern Europe. (Vickers, 2020) However, it never died out completely.

OTHER TYPES OF MAGIC

Galdr, seidr, and trolldom are some of the ancient magical practices that we have the most information on, but they are not the only ones that existed. You may hear of some of these others, so I'll give you a brief overview of a few. These tend to be more specific in their aim or in their technique than the ones we've discussed above. For example, remember the void which existed before the world began, Ginnungagap? There were those who believed the power of Ginnungagap could be drawn upon and wielded in magical practice, in particular in the calling forth of deities or other supernatural beings. This practice was called gandr. (Vickers, 2020)

While seidr is the most well-known form of divination magic, there was another type that was known as spæwork. This time of magic is based on the idea of "speaking" fate, whether by making prophecies or by allowing other beings, such as deities or ancestors, to speak through you. You can hear the same Germanic influence that we have in English in the name for this magic - it comes from "spæ", which translates into "to speak." (Knightly, n.d.j)

Lastly, there's the practice of ouitiseta, which involves spending the night, or many nights, somewhere out in nature that was believed to have a connection to magic or other worlds. These places would be holy sites like sacred tree groves or the mounds in which pre-Christian Norse peoples buried their dead. The idea was that these places are conduits of power, and by being in them, especially under the cover of dark night, you would become imbued with a greater power. (Vickers, 2020) This again illustrates the idea that "darkness" in Norse paganism is not seen as inherently bad, and indeed can be a source of great power.

KNOWLEDGE IS POWER

At this point, we haven't spoken much about specific rituals or other magical practices, but I hope you've started to understand a few key points of Norse magic: first, that there is no one way to do Norse magic. This is because no one can say for sure how these magics were originally done, and it is also because Norse paganism is based on philosophies which value individual circumstances and nuance over rules and doctrine.

And second, that knowledge - of yourself, of the world, and of the magic you're trying to invoke - is a huge part of Norse magic. That's why I've taken so long to lay the groundwork before jumping into things like rituals and rune work. I wanted you to have all the knowledge you might need - or at least, enough knowledge for you to know which direction to go should you need more. And now, in the next chapter, we'll get into how you might actually practice Norse magic in your everyday life.

CHAPTER 5
HOW TO BLÓT (AND OTHER RITUAL CONCERNS)

By this point in the book, I hope you've gotten the message that Norse paganism and magical practice is a thing that you can really make your own. Yes, there are some basic tenets (which we've just gone over) and yes, there are some ideas or methodologies that are more common than others. But for the most part, this is about finding out what works for you. And that's doubly important when it comes to the magical side of things, because magic happens at the point of interaction between you and the world. If you want your magic to be effective, you need to work on both sides of that equation. You need to seek to understand the world, but also, to understand yourself.

However, it can be just as frustrating to have no structure as it can to have too much structure, which is why through the years certain practices have developed. This includes a basic structure for blóts and other rituals, as well as some guidelines for common spiritual practices like veneration and working with deities. It also includes shared practices like holidays. You might think of holidays as time off work, or forced family bonding, or commercial gimmicks - and in many societies, they can be all those things. But holidays are also a chance to all acknowledge certain events or times of the year together. There is power in that kind of togetherness, and I'm going to give you a brief overview of the most common Norse pagan holidays so you'll be able to understand and experience that power.

Something to note is that not all Norse pagans are interested in magical practices, and that's fine. I assume that you are because, well, you're reading this book! But I mention this so you're aware that not everyone will practice all the things I mention in this chapter. Being respectful of other people's choices in regards to their practices is just good Norse pagan manners.

BEFORE YOU BEGIN

We're now at the point where you might want to start performing rituals, contacting deities, and otherwise engaging in magical acts. Before we get into any of that, it's important that you understand how to safely and effectively practice these types of magic. There are a few things I recommend you learn how to do before you act upon any of the other information in this chapter: cleansing, grounding, shielding, and warding.

Cleansing is about clearing away bad energy. This doesn't necessarily mean "evil" or "negative" energy - it might just be energy that is unhelpful or you otherwise would like to not have around. There are many ways to cleanse a space, some of which will be discussed later when we talk about consecration for a blót. You can cleanse with words, with sacred materials such as water and fire, and even with some sounds. The most important part of cleansing is that you are mentally prepared to push out unwanted energy. Your commitment is what will give the cleansing power. (Knightly, n.d.b)

Grounding is literally about renewing our connection with the ground. If you are not grounded you may feel disoriented or lifeless, because you're lacking the firmness and strength that we humans get from interacting with the earth. You can ground yourself by literally putting yourself into contact with the earth. You can also ground yourself through sensory experiences that will put your mind and body back in sync with each other, like eating, bathing, meditation, or dancing. (Wright, 2020)

Shielding and warding are both protective practices. Shielding can be as simple as mentally imagining a shield of energy around yourself, or as intricate as creating and wearing an amulet that you've imbued with protective intent. Warding is exactly the same, except wards are not meant to move with you, but to protect a specific space. You can make wards with words, with symbols, or with physical items such as amulets or crystals. (Knightly, n.d.b)

WORKING WITH THE GODS

The title of this section holds a clue to a crucial part of Norse deity work - you're going to work *with* the gods. Not under the gods, not for the gods, but with them. The Norse gods do not demand worship in the way that some other deities do. And Norse paganism is not a religion that requires you to interact with the gods in any one way. You do not need a designated holy book or an ordained cleric. And you don't have to maintain a certain level of formality - though of course, you can if you like. You can focus on just one deity in the Norse pantheon (known as "henotheism"); you can even include deities from other religions alongside Norse deities (known as "poly-affiliation"). To be frank, you don't have to work with any gods at all - though most of us do, because we find it fulfilling and helpful. (Knightly, n.d.n)

There are many different kinds of relationships that you can establish with your chosen deity. You might feel that a deity is a close friend, or perhaps a warm guiding presence that looks out for you like a parent might. You might learn from your deity, or you might be inspired by them to create or invent. The pluralism we've talked about extends to human-god relationships as well - there is no wrong way, and there might be several right ways. You might even have different kinds of relationships with different deities. (Knightly, n.d.b)

When you first start building a relationship with a god, you might not be sure where to begin. I recommend familiarizing yourself with the ways that gods can communicate with us. You can actively seek input from the gods with some forms of divination. Gods may choose to send you dreams or signs (usually called omens) that will indicate they want a relationship with you, and of what type. Some people find they have special senses, known as "clairsenses", which put them more in tune with the spiritual world. You are probably familiar with "clairvoyance", but there are many others. Some are like psychic enhancements of regular senses, others are particular skills such as empathy, getting premonitions, or artistic inspiration. (Knightly, n.d.b)

If you think you are making contact with a god, but are unsure, there are a few things you can do. You can request more omens. It's common practice to confirm omens with the rule of three - the idea that three similar occurrences are too much to be a coincidence. You should also always beware of any "god" whose wishes align too carefully with your own - our minds really love to convince us that we are being given the divine go-ahead to do whatever we want, when really we are just talking to ourselves. And you should never feel pressured to engage with any being that feels abusive, controlling, or otherwise likely to create an unhealthy relationship. (Knightly, n.d.b)

VENERATION

Veneration can be a great practice to cultivate in addition to more involved rituals. If you're not familiar with the idea of veneration - I wasn't when I first started - let me explain it. If we consult Merriam Webster, we'll find a basic but useful definition: "to honor (an icon, a relic, etc.) with a ritual act of devotion" (Merriam-Webster, n.d.) So veneration is any action that you perform regularly and intentionally to honor someone or something. Usually in Norse paganism, the object of your devotion will be a god or an ancestor. (Ancestor veneration is like any other form of veneration, it just centers your own forebears instead of a god or other being.)

One form of veneration will probably be familiar to most people, regardless of their religious background: praying. You can pray in any way that you see fit - some people prefer to make up their own prayers, while others like to rely on books, manuscripts like the Eddas, or even Google searches to find prayers that resonate with them. Another way you can venerate a deity or ancestor is to perform an activity in their honor. This could be something that you are particularly skilled at, such as a creative endeavor, or it could be something connected to the deity, such as studying in honor of Odin. (Knightly, n.d.c)

Choosing who to venerate is a very personal decision. It doesn't have to be one of the "big" gods - in fact, Norse beliefs kind of eschew the idea that there is such a thing. Yes, there are well-known gods, and yes, the ones like Odin and Thor have a lot of power. But part of the animistic worldview is that everything has some spark of divinity, and we can be drawn to "smaller" beings as much as any other. In fact, sometimes these more local entities will be more responsive and helpful because our connection to them will be stronger. (Knightly, n.d.n)

TO BLÓT OR NOT TO BLÓT

That heading is actually just a joke, because it's almost certain that you are going to perform or attend a blót (probably many) as part of your Norse magic practice. To refresh your memory, "blót" is an umbrella term for any kind of spiritual ritual in heathenry or Norse paganism. It can be anything from a formal ceremony to a quiet offering at your home altar. The key point to keep in mind about blóts is they are meant to connect us to greater forces - to our pagan communities, to the Norse deities, to our ancestors, and to the wide web of magic and wyrd that exists in the world. (Knightly, n.d.l)

In ancient and medieval times, there were a lot of common rituals that were designed to keep us connected to each other and to the world, both natural and mystical, that we live in. Many of these were acts of balance, meant to restore equilibrium to the world by making offerings in exchange for the things that we had received. You can see this kind of thinking in present-day Norse paganism and magic, as we discussed in depth with the gifting cycle. Modern societies, especially the very capitalistic ones, tend to see exchanges as acts of selfishness - you scratch my back, I'll scratch yours. But the Norse way is to see exchanges as an act of balance. A blót is centered around this act of balance; you will enter into communion with a spirit, and offer them something either in supplication for a request or in thanks for a blessing.

All blóts will involve an offering of some sort. Perhaps the most common offering is some sort of drink. A liquid offering can be both drunk by those joining the blót and poured out in honor of and sacrifice for a deity or other spiritual being. No element of the blót is particularly mystical or serious (especially in modern times, when we no longer practice blood sacrifices). Instead, it is the working of all the elements together that elevates these casual actions such as speaking and drinking into something more. (Kornevall, 2021)

LOCATION, LOCATION, LOCATION

Before you can actually get to any blóts, there's something very important you'll need - a place to perform them. Blóts have been and are performed in many different types of locations. There is no specific place where you need to be to perform one, and when I walk you through how to perform a blót, the first thing we'll cover is how to consecrate any area where you find yourself. There are, however, a couple of specific places where you might find yourself attending a blót, particularly if you choose to practice in a more communal setting.

The first location to know about is a "lund." This is a grove of trees, usually sacred ones like oak or ash. The next is a "haug" or "barrow", which is a burial mound. We've discussed how burial mounds were believed to be magical spaces, so it makes sense that blóts would be performed here. When possible, many Norse pagans still prefer to practice in these outdoor settings, as we know the early Norse peoples did. Sometimes, however, due to weather or other deterrents, blóts will take place indoors. When this happens, the building where a blót is performed is called a "hov." (Kornevall, 2021)

The last location I want to discuss is your personal altar. An altar is a space you've designated in your home as the location where you will perform rituals and magical acts. (Altars are sometimes referred to as "shrines", but I avoid this so as not to confuse altars with the type of shrine where a spiritual being resides when visiting your home.) Altars should contain elements that are important to you, such as representations of your chosen deities or forebears that you want to venerate. There can be some elements of your altar that change with the seasons, such as greenery or other natural elements. This is also the place where you will leave offerings from your personal blóts - commonly food and drink, and possibly also small gifts. (Knightly, n.d.c)

Note: It is also possible to build an altar outside your home. This is usually done with stones that you've collected. A stone altar is called a "harg" or a "cairn." (Kornevall, 2021) Once you've built this altar, you can leave it and return to it, so this is an excellent idea if you have an outdoor space that you frequent and like to use for your rituals.

YOUR FIRST BLÓT

The most basic blót procedure follows seven steps: first, consecrate or hallow the space where you will have the blót; second, focus your mind; third, invoke the deities, ancestors, or other spirits you wish to commune with; fourth, declare your purpose and your offering (why you're performing the blót, what you wish to get from it, and what you are offering in return); five, perform the blessing; six, give your offering; and seven, close (end) the blót. (Asatru Community, n.d.) Let's look at each of these steps in a little bit more detail.

Consecration: Also called hallowing, consecrating a space makes it holy and protects it from influences that might harm you or cloud your focus while you perform the ritual. (This is not necessary if you are performing the ritual at your own altar.) Some common forms of consecration are via a holy substance (mead, fire), through an incantation or supplication to a deity to banish any bad influences - Thor is a good choice, for his strength, or the local land spirits who have a connection with the location. (Härger, 2016)

Some people also like to make the sign of Thor's hammer (an upside-down T) in each of the four cardinal directions before calling upon Thor's protection. (Asatru Community, n.d.) If you prefer, you can borrow from some other pagan faiths with practices like drawing a circle (which offers extra protection), sweeping the area clean with a broom, or clearing the air by smudging or fanning swan feathers. (Kornevall, 2021)

Focus: Now that you've created a sacred area in physical space, you'll want to take care of your headspace, too. You always want to enter a blót with a clear and focused mind, in order to best connect with the spiritual forces at work. There are several ways to do this, and you should choose the one that works best for you. Some people like to chant, to sing, or to perform a reading from one of the Eddas. (Asatru Community, n.d.) For others, meditation and breathing exercises help to center and ground them.

This might also be a time to spiritually bring together all who are partaking in the blót. Some people like to have everyone involved in a blót take an oath that they will maintain harmony among one another for the duration of the blót. If the participants know one another well, this can also be a time to address past disputes and resolve them, in order to go into the ceremony with a clear conscious and a renewed sense of

Invocation: Another term for the invocation is the "calling", because it is about calling out to the spirits that you're hoping to meet during the blót. This literally involves calling the names of the deities, ancestors, or other beings. Often people will face north while doing the invocation. (Asatru Community, n.d.) You can do this however you like, with traditional calls or ones of your own writing, with spoken word or even with song. It's important to remember that this call is not a command - we do not command the gods. Rather, it is a request. (Härger, 2016)

Purpose: This part of the blót is kind of two parts in one. First, you give an explanation for the ceremony. This action goes by many names. It might be called the advice, the rede, or the council. (Härger, 2016) All you need to do is state, in words however simple or fancy that you like, why you're here and what you hope to achieve. You'll follow this with preparing your sacrifice, and then offering it to the gods. It is common to also state aloud what you have brought to be exchanged for your request. (Asatru Community, n.d.)

Blessing: This is the part of the blót where you bless the offering you've brought. There is a lot of variety in performing a blessing, in part because there are many acceptable ways to do it, and there can also be many different types of offerings (drink, food, small objects, etc.) The best way to choose how to perform the blessing is to research your type of offering. Once you have infor-mation on the possibilities, you can choose your method based on what you are drawn to and what works best with the request you are making.

Offering: Now you want to actually offer up your sacrifice. Again, there are many ways you might do this. A very common one is to offer ale or mead by pouring it out on the ground, where the gods can accept it. (Asatru Community, n.d.) For food offerings, you might bury it or sink it in water, or leave it for wild animals. (Härger, 2016) Remember to always be respectful of nature, and not to leave anything that would harm plants or animals, or upset the natural balance of a place.

Closing: The purpose of the closing step is just to give the ritual a definitive ending. This is important mentally for the participants, and also will allow the energy that has gathered throughout the blót to be dispersed. You can speak a few simple words (or many flowery ones, if that's your preference), or even do a chant or song. (Härger, 2016) Just as with other parts of the blót, you can write your own closing or you can research those written by others. After closing the blót, it can be nice to have a meal with the other participants. You can include the gods you just invoked in the meal by leaving a portion of food for them at the table or on your altar. (Kornevall, 2021)

THROWING A SUMBEL

The above is a great structure for blóts, especially when you're just starting out. But it isn't the only form a blót can take. For example, a sumbel is a celebratory kind of blót which is based on a ceremony described in Beowulf, one of the most well-known epic poems written in Old English. Sumbels revolve around drinking together and making an offering of the libations - each person will toast and then drink, pass to the next person, and so on and so forth. Traditionally this goes for several rounds, sometimes with each round dedicated to a particular type of toast or offering (one round for the gods, one round for oath-taking, etc.) Within this basic framework, you can vary the sumbel to suit your purposes. (Knightly, n.d.l)

For example, you could have a college graduation sumbel, which might in many ways resemble a typical graduation party with themed party plates and streamers in your school colors - except for a portion of the evening, you drink toasts to Odin for guiding your wisdom and Thor for lending you strength; to your professors and fellow students for their role in your education; and in honor of your late grandfather who's dream it was to see you graduate. Or for another example, you could have a subtler celebration in which a few friends come over to celebrate your moving into a new house; here you might use a fancy goblet and drink toasts to Freyr for bringing you prosperity and to Freyja in hopes she will bless you with children to fill the home.

AS THE WHEEL (OF THE YEAR) TURNS

In addition to your own sacred rituals, there may be times when you wish to celebrate with others. This could mean physically with others, in communal celebrations, or it could simply mean that you wish to mark the same occasions that you know others are also celebrating. I like to do this because even if I'm not physically present with other people, it gives me a sense of connection. The calendar of the pagan holidays is often called the Wheel of the Year, highlighting that these celebrations are part of the cyclical nature of life, ever-changing but always coming around again, moving from life to death, from light to dark, from warmth to cold, and then back again, eternally.

Some Norse pagans will celebrate holidays from the solar calendar or the lunar calendar - or both. It is common for certain regions or organizations to celebrate the same holidays, in order to foster a sense of community. While there are no set holidays that you must celebrate, it is very rare for a Norse pagan to not celebrate

Jül (the winter solstice) and Midsummer (the summer solstice). (Knightly, n.d.i)

As with many winter solstice celebrations, Jül marks the point in the year when the sun begins to return to us. The solstice is the shortest day of the year, and after it passes, the days begin to grow longer again. Jül is also known as Midwinter, and the celebration for Jül is called Jülblót. Odin is a big part of Jül celebrations and takes on a special form called the Jülfather, and Frejya is also strongly associated with Jül. Another well-known part of Scandinavian midwinter celebrations is the tradition of women and girls going from house to house with candles (symbolic of the returning sun) and gifts. This tradition merged with Christianity in the form of St. Lucia. (Kornevall, 2021)

Can you guess what the midsummer celebration is called? It's a pretty obvious one - it's called "Midsommarblót." It celebrates the opposite point in the solar cycle from midwinter, when the days are longest and the sun is strongest, just before the sun's strength starts to wane. It is common to celebrate midsummer with drinks and dancing, including dancing around the Maypole - another tradition Norse paganism shares with other pagan cultures. (Kornevall, 2021) In the Ásatrú tradition, midsummer is known as Þingblót, a festival of light and order, celebrating the rule of law in addition to the summer solstice. (Staff IM, 2019) Light in the Norse tradition is often linked with order, which should make sense to you if you remember that the Aesir themselves are gods of both light and order.

There are other major festivals in some Norse pagan traditions. For example, Icelandic Ásatrú followers usually celebrate Sigurblót and Veturnáttablót in addition to Jül and Midsummer. Sigurblót celebrates the coming of spring and the god Freyr. And Veturnáttablót celebrates the end of fall and the start of winter. It is associated with Odin. (Staff IM, 2019) Other traditions will celebrate similar holidays that are linked to the spring and fall equinoxes. (NMD, n.d.d) No matter the specifics, all these celebrations are deeply connected to the seasons and the life cycle of the natural world. They reflect the origins of Norse magic as part of an animistic religion that believes many parts of the world are sacred.

Some other blóts you may hear about or see celebrated include:

Disablót, which is a celebration of the feminine and the slowly warming earth held in February; Segerblót, which marks your survival through the winter and can be held any time after Disablót and before Vårblot; Vårblot, which is celebrated in March for the coming of spring and the growth of new plants; Majblót, a May celebration for the start of summer (similar to the more well-known May Day); Sensommarblót and Höstblót, harvest festivals held in toward the beginning and end of harvest season, respectively; and Alvablót, held around the same time as Halloween and a festival to honor the dead, including our ancestors and those that left us in the past year. (Kornevall, 2021)

One final note about holidays: As noted, many of these are based on natural phenomena such as the seasons and the solar calendar. This can mean that you want to change the timing of your holidays to match the seasons if you live in a place where the climate or the timing is very different from northern Europe. Or, you can always choose to retain the traditional schedule, knowing that your weather might not match, but you are in tune with many other pagans practicing in various parts of the world. Whichever works for you is the one you should choose!

CHAPTER 6

HAMMERS, RAVENS, AND SPEARS, OH MY

B efore we leave the general practice of magic and dive into the world of runes and divination, I want to take a chapter to introduce another important part of Norse magic - symbols. For some, these symbols will have magical properties in and of themselves; for others, they are simply visual reminders of their beliefs and of the magical world that surrounds us all. From carvings on ancient graves to tattoos on modern pagans, symbols have always been an important part of Norse culture.

The early Norse people might not have been big on keeping records, but they loved a good story. Many of the symbols in this chapter were born from those stories, as illustrations that condensed well-known tales such as the Eddas, the sagas, and other myths into simple visual clues, instantly recognizable to those in the know. We've already discussed one of the most well-known Norse symbols, which is the world tree Yggdrasil. Some of the others I've mentioned in passing, such as Thor's hammer Mjölnir, while others I'll introduce to you for the first time in this chapter.

Some of the symbols I'll discuss here are very, very old - thousands of years BCE. Others are only a few hundred years old. This is because through the centuries, Scandinavian culture and the belief systems that it inspired have collected more and more symbols. There may be some people who are only interested in "traditional" symbols, while others are more open to all types of symbols. Once again, the beauty of Norse magic as a belief system is that it does not have to be the same for all people. Particularly if you are hoping to gain some magical benefit from a symbol, such as protection or wisdom, the most important thing to consider is whether or not the symbol speaks to you.

MJÖLNIR, THOR'S HAMMER

Mjölnir is Thor's magical hammer, which was related to his ability to command thunder, lightning, and storms. Mjölnir was created by the dwarves but Loki cunningly convinced them to give it to Thor. Mjölnir was known to be so powerful that it could knock down a mountain, so it's no wonder that both past and modern pagans want to invoke its power. (Rogador, 2020a) In the stories of Thor's exploits, Mjölnir always went where Thor aimed, and once it had found its target, it would come back to Thor's hand. (Wigington, 2019a)

As a protective symbol, the hammer was carved over doors or on gravestones. Amulets were also created as small pendants usually made of antler, bone, or bronze. (Rogador, 2020a) As an amulet, Mjölnir is believed to protect its bearer. It was a very popular symbol throughout history and has been found in various designs in Denmark, Iceland, Norway, and Sweden. (Wigington, 2019a) Archeologists have discovered the largest amount of Mjölnir amulets in the period right after Christianity became the dominant religion in Scandinavia, indicating that pagans who did not wish to convert were seeking small ways to hold onto their pagan beliefs. (Mark, 2019)

Mjölnir was also associated with fertility, which explains why you might see it used at weddings or in the homes of couples hoping to conceive. (Mark, 2019) While the hammer is used in many Norse pagan traditions, it is worth noting that it has in some cases been co-opted by white supremacists. This of course does not mean you cannot use it - you can and should. Just be aware that in some cases, white supremacist or Nazi imagery like the swastika will be snuck into this symbol. (ADL, n.d.a)

HUGINN & MUNINN, ODIN'S RAVENS

When we first discussed Odin, I mentioned he had two ravens that he sent around the world to gather information for him. The ravens were named Huginn (which means thought) and Muninn (which means memory). (Mark, 2019) Huginn and Muninn can be found on many objects with many purposes - everything from armor to jewelry to kitchenware. (Traylor, 2019) Among the symbolic meanings of these ravens, one of the more obvious and prominent ones was as the physical embodiments of Odin's wisdom and desire for knowledge.

However, due to Odin's roles on the battlefield and in the halls of Valhalla, they were also associated with symbols of death. Because of this, representations of Huginn and Muninn were also often used in funeral decorations, such as on urns. (Mark, 2019) In our modern era, Odin's ravens have found other symbolic positions, including joining characters like Thor and Odin in the world of superhero comics, and inspiring the name of an Italian black metal band. (Traylor, 2019) Not to mention, the idea of ravens as both as wise and tricky, and as omens for death or dark times, is so prevalent now as to often transcend the association with Norse mythology altogether.

GUNGNIR, ODIN'S SPEAR

Gungnir is the name of Odin's spear, which like Thor's hammer was not just a weapon but an emblem inspired by that weapon.

Also like Mjölnir, it was a magical creation of the dwarves, with the ability to always influence the battle in Odin's favor. There are various stories about the creation of Gungnir. Perhaps it was made out of the light from the sun (this would explain why it was said to look like a falling star when Odin threw it) - or maybe, it was made out of wood taken from the world tree itself. Like Mjölnir with Thor, Gungnir never fails to hit where Odin has aimed it. (Rogador, 2020c)

Interestingly, Gungnir was not just drawn or carved symbolically - an actual spear would be the first weapon used by Vikings at the start of a battle, in hopes of honoring Odin and therefore turning the battle in the Vikings' favor. (Mark, 2019) In addition to (hopefully) helping to win battles, oaths could be sworn on Gungnir. This is believed to be because the spear was so powerful and its bond to Odin was so strong. (Rogador, 2020c)

THE TRIPLE HORN OF ODIN

This symbol is what's known as a triskelion, which means that it is made up of three identical and overlapping pieces. The triple horn is a very old symbol, dating back to at least 3200 BCE. (Rogador, 2020b) It might remind you of other triskelions, such as the Celtic knot, which has become rather ubiquitous in recent years. The three pieces in this case are three curved lines, each representing Odin's drinking horn. Odin was associated with the drinking of a mead that was made from the blood of the god Kvasir, who was very wise and skilled in poetry. In the legend, Odin was able to get three drinks of this mead, and the three horns are said to symbolize those three drinks. Because of this association, the triple horn can mean wisdom and may be used as a symbol by bards and other poets. (Wigington, 2019a)

The three horns can also symbolize different elements, such as earth, water, and sky, and different planes of existence, such as the physical world, the spiritual world, and the celestial world.

(Rogador, 2020b) By now you may have noticed the number three repeats itself quite a bit in Norse mythology and therefore in Norse magic. Many cultures and religions hold the number three to be particularly divine, and Norse culture is no exception. While obviously Odin is a masculine god, the function of the horns as drinking vessels is sometimes also linked to the divine feminine aspect associated with vessels. (Wigington, 2019a)

VALKNUT, THE WARRIOR'S KNOT

Another triskelion symbol, the valknut is made up of three triangles that are woven together. This symbol is also connected to Odin, and can often be found in company with ravens and wolves. The connection with Odin makes sense, because the name means "slain warrior's knot", and those warriors who died in battle were thought to join Odin in Valhalla. Fittingly, it can also be called "Odin's Knot." Not much is known about the deeper meaning behind the valknut, but the prominence of threes (three triangles, themselves made up of three sides and three corners) and the significance of them being woven together, as the fates of the world are woven together, are often thought to be key points. (Berloga Workshop, 2019)

Because of the association with Odin and soldiers killed in battle, the valknut can be seen as an emblem of passing from life to death. It can also be a binding symbol, in reference to Odin's powers and his ability to release the dead from one life and guide them to the next. There is another, slightly more controversial interpretation of the valknut, which is that it is meant to depict the heart of the giant Hrungnir. Hrungnir's heart was a stone that had three corners, so you can see why some scholars believe the valknut represents it. However, others believe that this is just a coincidental similarity, and that the number three is found in both simply due to its popularity in the religion as a whole. (Mark, 2019) Unfortunately, like Mjölnir, the valknut has been adopted by some white supremacist groups, so be wary of that when you encounter it in the wild. (ADL, n.d.b)

AEGISHJALMUR, THE HELM OF AWE

As you might have guessed from the word helm, this symbol resembles a shield. Specifically, it is a circular shield with pronged branches (usually eight of them) reaching outward from the middle. The branches, sometimes called tridents, are similar to a protective rune, and the number (eight) is thought to represent the eight legs of Odin's magical horse Sleipnir. (Mark, 2019) While eight is the most common number of branches or arms, the number can vary, as can the way they're laid out on the circle. It's possible the prongs along the branches are also based on a rune, one that is speculated to have a connection with ice and the jötnar. (McCoy, n.d.c)

Like Thor's hammer, the helm is a depiction of a specific object - this time, a helm won from Fafnir the dragon by the dragonslayer Sigurd in both the Poetic and Prose Eddas. (Mark, 2019) The helm gave both the dragon and Sigurd great power when they wielded it, and as a symbol, the helm was used to ensure victory for its wielder. (McCoy, n.d.c)

VEGVISIR, THE ANCIENT COMPASS

If you're unfamiliar, you may confuse the vegvisir with the helm of awe, as both feature eight branches radiating out from a central point. One of the ways you can distinguish the vegvisir from the helm of awe is the points on the helm of awe are all the same, while those on the vegvisir are all different. (Hogarth, 2020) In the vegvisir, these branches represent the eight directions (the four cardinal directions and the four intermediate ones). Its name comes from the combining of Norse words meaning "path" and "guide." If you're thinking that the vegvisir is a lot like a compass, you're not wrong. Because it is believed to guide your path, this symbol is used often for safety and by travelers, though of course it can also bear the meaning of guidance in the intellectual or spiritual sense.

The version of the symbol as we know it is not particularly old, having first been in widespread use in the 19th century. Whether or not this version was based on or inspired by older versions now lost to time is unknown. (Eds., n.d.) In addition to amulets and other physical forms of the vegvisir, it was also sometimes drawn directly on the body of the person it was meant to protect - most commonly, on the person's forehead. Allegedly, this was originally done ceremonially with blood, but of course we have no actual records or evidence to prove this claim. Nowadays, many people get tattoos made of the vegvisir (perhaps most famously, Icelandic musician Björk has a vegvisir arm tattoo). (Hogarth, 2020)

SVENTHORN, THE THORN THAT PUTS YOU TO SLEEP

The name "sventhorn" translates into "sleep thorn", and it has a straightforward interpretation: a visual depiction of sleep-inducing thorns that would incapacitate your target by making them fall fast asleep. The sventhorn might be the Norse symbol that is most obviously magical - and not just because it sounds like something a fairy tale princess might accidentally prick her finger on. Both the actual sventhorn and symbolic depictions of it are described with the ability to either make someone sleep or keep them from waking. (Mark, 2019)

There is significant variation in how the sventhorn is depicted, and also in how to best deploy this symbol. In the myths is it a physical object, taking various pointed forms such as a spear or arrow, that the enemy is hit with in order to render them unconscious. At times it seems to have acted for a set amount of time; in other tales, it lasts indefinitely so long as the thorn remains in the victim's body. Some spells from Icelandic sources have suggested more symbolic methods of deploying the sventhron, including a carving placed under the target's head while sleeping. (McCoy, n.d.k)

OTHER SYMBOLS

These are some of the most common symbols found in Norse history, mythology, and magic, but there are many others. In addition to his ravens, his horns, and his spear, Odin also had his eight-legged horse and two wolves named Geri and Freki. These animals were also sometimes used as symbols in the same way that the ravens were. And we already learned about the idea of the web of wyrd when we discussed wyrd and orlog in chapter four. A simple rendition of the web of wyrd is often used as a symbol of connection and destiny. Other symbols include the trollkors ("troll cross") and the Viking ax. At one point the swastika was also a quite common symbol throughout Europe, though it is mostly avoided now for obvious reasons. (Rogador, 2021)

And of course, there's another type of symbol that has come up a few times in this chapter - runes. Runes are symbols in the sense that all letters are symbols, written depictions of words and thoughts for the purpose of communication. They are also symbols that can be added to other symbols, as discussed above with the helm of awe. And lastly, the runes will sometimes stand alone, as each rune has its own meaning. Runes are, in my opinion, the coolest part of Norse magic, and I'm excited to teach you all about them in the next two chapters.

CHAPTER 7
LETTERS AND SECRETS

The word rune is found throughout the Germanic languages of the world, and in each of those languages, it holds a dual meaning. The first meaning is "letter", and the second meaning is "secret", sometimes translated as "mystery." (McCoy, n.d.h) This etymological tidbit is very telling, because on the one hand, runes were (and are) letters just like the Latin letters you're reading right now. On the other hand, individual runes have symbolic and mystical meanings that our modern alphabets are largely lacking. This chapter will take you through the history of runes, as well as the structure of the runic alphabet, what we know about how they were used by early Norse peoples, and a little bit about how we use them today.

Runes are first and foremost a writing system. This is the one use and meaning that all scholars and pagan practitioners agree on. Runes were the first alphabets (that we know of) that were used by early Norse civilizations. (McCoy, n.d.h) Their use pre-dates the use of the Latin alphabet in Scandinavia. You may have seen the runic alphabets referred to as "futhark", which is a designation that comes from the six letters at the beginning of the runic alphabet. In fact, "futhark" is for runes the equivalent of "alphabet", because both words come from the first letters of their respective writing systems. (McKay, 2021) (Note that the "th" in this is the Latin equivalent - in runes, this is one letter, the symbol "Þ." If you ever see the word "Þor", know that it is a hybrid word using both alphabets. Translate the "Þ" to "th" and you get: "Thor"!)

ODIN ON THE TREE AND TRADERS ON THE ELBE - HOW RUNES BEGAN

There are several theories as to what person or group of people first created the writing system we now know as the Norse runes. It might have been mercenary soldiers in the Roman army. Or it could have been traders who wanted to further facilitate their commerce by adding to their tools for communication. Whoever first "invented" the runes, it is widely believed that they first developed from writing systems that had migrated northward from southern European tribes. These would have been alphabets from the Italian peninsula, and those alphabets would have been based on the one used by the Greeks. (McKay, 2021)

This migration likely happened through military engagement, when warriors from northern European tribes ventured south in search of more people to fight. These systems would have been adopted and adapted, and probably combined with meaningful symbols already in use. The association of the runes with Odin may have started here, as Odin was also the war god who would have been supplicated for victory. (McCoy, n.d.g) There is also an alternate theory, which suggests that the systems of writing were spread by tribes of nomads who moved up and down the Elbe River in what is present-day Germany. (McKay, 2021)

Of course, the mythological explanation for the existence of runes is a bit different. One of the most well-known stories of Norse mythology is that of Odin seeking to understand the mysteries of the runes. Before Odin's sacrifice on the tree, no one - not humans, but also not the gods - could read the runes.

(Brethauer, n.d.) The price of understanding, Odin was told, was to hang on a tree for nine days and nights without food or water. He paid it, and was rewarded with the knowledge of the runes, which he then shared with mankind. (Wigington, 2019c) While the historic and mythological origins of the runes may seem at odds, I want to point out that both have at their core a desire for greater connection and understanding. Odin's thirst for knowledge can be seen to symbolically represent the expansion of the medieval world as different cultures made contact with one another, melding their societies through trade and conquest.

CARVED IN STONE AND... CHURCH BELLS?

As with other early Norse history, the information we have on the use of runes comes from later sources whose accuracy cannot be verified. However, runes possessed one characteristic that most other elements of early Norse life did not - they were written down. This means that in addition to what people said and say about the runes, we have the runes themselves. From translations of runic inscriptions, we can see that runes were a means of communicating a variety of sentiments. (Knightly, n.d.m)

Remember that the early Norse societies passed along much of their knowledge orally, so you wouldn't find them making books of stories from the myths, or sending letters to one another. So when they did break out their writing system, you knew it was for something important. (McKay, 2021) And while runes were sometimes literally written down, with ink on paper, it was far more common for runes to be inscribed on objects. Most of the runic inscriptions we've found from pre-Christian northern Europe have been used in this way, to mark objects for memorial purposes, for identification, or sometimes to charge an item with magic. (Knightly, n.d.m)

The fact that you would often be engraving these characters into a substance such as wood or stone, or sometimes bone and metal, is perhaps why they are made up of straight lines - much easier to carve than curved lines. (McCoy, n.d.h) One of the most common categories of these rune-inscribed objects would be what's called a "runestone." You can guess from the name what a runestone is: a stone that has been carved with runes. These were sometimes boulders that were already freestanding, or chunks of stone that had to be hewn out of bedrock. In keeping with the most common use of runes themselves, runestones were most often used to commemorate fallen soldiers or other well-known figures. (Atkins, 2018) The number of runestones that have been found in the northern parts of Europe numbers in the thousands. (Wigington, 2019c)

Most of the runestones that have been found are believed to have been carved between 800 CE and 1000 CE - though the earliest ones may date back to the 300s, as is the case with the runestone in Rakkestad, Norway, which uses runes to write in an early Germanic language that predates even Old Norse. We know exactly what some of these runestones say, while others still evade translation. There are even different styles of carving runes into runestones, such as Ringerike. Ringerike is a decorative way of carving runes by adding animal heads, often those of snakes or other intimidating animals, to the end of a band of runes. This type of carving is named after Ringerike in Norway, where the first set of runestones carved in this manner was found. (Nikel, 2020)

There are many beautiful and mysterious runestones spread throughout Scandinavia that can still be visited today. There is the five-sided Viking runestone in Rök, Sweden, a memorial with over 700 runes carved into it. It makes note of the death of its carver's son, and also perhaps commemorates the period of extreme cold that medieval Sweden was going through at the time of its carving. Another well-known Swedish runestone is the Stenkvista runestone, which speaks of Thor and bears a carving of his hammer. There are also two famous runestones in Jelling, Denmark. These sit near burial mounds, and one of them was put up by Harald

Bluetooth, the king whose name would later be the inspiration for the name of "bluetooth" technology. (Nikel, 2020)

Runes continued to be used in Scandinavia even after Christianity became the dominant religion. They have even been found on objects such as church bells or incense containers. The use of runes in Christian churches is another example of the ways that pagan and Christian life blended together - Christian teachings were likely inscribed into runic lines that would be easier to read for the newly converted. (NMD, n.d.f) In addition to appropriation by Christians, runes were also maintained in some calendars. Runes were attached to certain holidays and other important events. (Knightly, n.d.m) They were also used in agriculture as a way of stamping produce. In some places, runes were still being used in these ways well into the 1900s. (McKay, 2021)

HOW TO USE RUNES (HINT: THERE'S NOT JUST ONE WAY.)

On a nuts and bolts level, runes work much the same as modern alphabets, where each rune stands for a sound - in linguistic terms, a "phoneme." One interesting point brought up by Daniel McCoy in his discussion of runes is the linguistic theory of phonosematism. This theory suggests that the sounds of a word are not random, but rather have some inherent quality that, when put together, aurally signifies the quality of the word being formed. McCoy suggests that this theory works especially well with Norse runes and the early Norse cultures, where words were believed to have inherent power. (McCoy, n.d.i) Within this framing, all parts of the rune have significance. The way it's drawn, the way it sounds, and even its name, all work together to manifest meaning.

Modern usage of runes has gone through many changes, and at times branched off depending on the purposes of the magician. You may hear about Guido Von List, who unfortunately developed a system of rune use to accompany his "Aryan" religion early in the 1900s. There was also Ralph Blum, who wrote a book in the 1980s claiming to teach how to read the future with runes. Blum devised a system that was based on information about runes from old sources combined with principles of divination from other sources, such as the Chinese text "I-Ching." (Knightly, n.d.m) Blum's biggest "authentic" sources were rune poems - poems found in England, Iceland, and Norway that detail the names and meanings of the runes. He incorporated the information from those poems into his own invented structure for rune magic. (McCoy, n.d.h)

Earlier in this chapter I mentioned the king Harold Bluetooth, and in the beginning of the book I mentioned the symbol inspired by his name as an example of how ancient Norse culture subtly exists all around us today. That symbol is a combination of two runes, what is called a "bindrune." Unfortunately, we have no evidence that bindrunes had any significance in early Norse civilization, outside of a decorative effect similar to the embellishments seen in illuminated manuscripts. Bindrunes could absolutely have been used for mystical purposes - it's just not something we can prove. The methods we have today of using bindrunes in magical contexts have been developed by modern pagans. (Knightly, n.d.m)

As rune usage changed and spread throughout history, more than one version of the runic system developed. Sometimes letters would change sounds, adapting to the way the sounds of Norse languages were changing. (McKay, 2021) Today, we recognize three main futharks, known as the Elder, the Anglo-Saxon, and the Younger Futharks. (Knightly, n.d.m) The Elder Futhark, as you might guess, is the oldest of these alphabets, created between 0 and 400 CE. The Younger Futhark succeeded it in Scandinavian countries, while the Anglo-Saxon Futhark came after it in England. (McCoy, n.d.h) The Anglo-Saxon futhark is at times referred to as "Futhorc", because of the differences in the letters between the two systems. (McKay, 2021)

There were also other runic alphabets - with varying degrees of similarity to the three futharks - found in Etruria, Turkey, and Hungary. (Wigington, 2019c) Early discoveries of runes include inscriptions on a brooch found in what is now northern Germany, dated to 50 CE; a comb found in Denmark, dated to 160 CE, and a spearhead found in Norway, also dated to around 160 CE. The brooch inscription has never been conclusively identified as Norse runes, but the comb and spear have. Additionally, the entire Elder Futhark was discovered carved into a stone found in Sweden and dated to 400 CE. (McCoy, n.d.g)

For the rest of this chapter, I'll focus on the Elder Futhark, as it's the oldest and therefore the closest to those used by the early Norse pagans. It is the futhark that I use most often, and one of the most commonly used in runic magic. (Though of course, if you are interested in the other futharks, I encourage you to do your own research - there are certainly resources out there.)

WHAT'S IN A NAME?

Each letter in the Elder Futhark has a name. If you think about it, our letters have names, too. If I write A, B, C, D, E, F, G, you probably read each of those letter's names, right? (And maybe got a certain alphabet song stuck in your head - my apologies.) But a rune's name was more than just a label that was useful if you needed to spell a word. It would often contain within it the sound the rune makes and the story behind the rune's design. Often runes would be linked to particular gods - their names would be similar to the god's name, and their design would indicate something about the god's power. (McCoy, n.d.h)

The following chart will show you the names of the Elder Futhark runes as well as the meaning of each name, and the way the rune is pronounced. (These names and meanings are as found in the rune poems I mentioned above and compiled in English by author Daniel McCoy on his website Norse Mythology for Smart People.) Keep in mind that a rune's name has a meaning, and the rune itself will also have a symbolic meaning, which we will discuss a bit later.

Rune	Sounds Like	Name	Name Meaning
ᚠ	f	"fehu"	cattle
ᚢ	u	"uruz"	aurochs (an extinct kind of wild ox)
ᚦ	th	"thurisaz"	giant
ᚨ	a	"ansuz"	one of the Aesir gods
ᚱ	r	"raidho"	to travel by horseback
ᚲ	k	"kaunan"	ulcer
ᚷ	g	"gebo"	gift
ᚹ	w	"wunjo"	joy
ᚺ	h	"hagalaz"	hail (as in the weather phenomenon)
ᚾ	n	"naudhiz"	need
ᛁ	i	"isaz"	ice
ᛃ	j	"jera"	year
ᛇ	i ('eye')	"eihwaz"	yew
ᛈ	p	name unknown	meaning unknown
ᛉ	z	name unknown	meaning unknown
ᛊ	s	"sowilo"	sun
ᛏ	t	"Tiwaz"	referencing the god Tiwaz
ᛒ	b	"berkanan"	birch
ᛖ	e	"ehwaz"	horse
ᛗ	m	"mannaz"	man
ᛚ	l	"laguz"	meaning unknown
ᛜ	ng	"Ingwaz"	referencing the god Ingwaz
ᛟ	o	"othalan"	inheritance
ᛞ	d	"dagaz"	day

Notice how the first letter or sound of each rune's name also corresponds with the sound it makes - this can help you out when you're first learning the runes. Another thing that helped me when I was first learning the runes was to focus on one Aett at a time. An

Aett is a group of runes, often thought of as a type of "family." There are three Aettir in the Elder Futhark, and each is associated with one of the Aesir: Freyja, Heimdall, and Tyr.

Freyja's Aettir encompasses the first eight runes: ᚠᚢᚦᚨᚱᚲᚷᚹ

Heimdall's Aettir is the next eight: ᚺᚾᛁᛋᛃᛈᛇᛉᛊ

And Tyr's Aettir is the final eight: ᛏᛒᛖᛗᛚᛜᛞᛟᚾ

Each Aett is loosely based around a theme. Freyja's, being first, focuses on things that were of great value to the early Norse people. This includes animals and other things associated with livelihood, as well as abstract concepts such as joy. Heimdall's is about strength, protection, balancing forces (opposites), and elemental forces (such as ice and the sun). Tyr's Aett contains his rune (Tiwaz), of course, as well as that of the god Ingwaz (another name for Freyr). Other runes in his Aett deal with archetypal characters (man, horse) and ideas of societal order like days and inheritance. (Siofra, 2021)

These categories may not always seem logical or make sense to us, perhaps because of the information that we've lost over time. However, I found that even if I didn't understand why each rune was in its group, having that structure made it much easier to learn and remember the names and meanings of the runes. Three families of runes that "live" together are much easier to approach than a list of 24 runes all at once, which can feel overwhelming.

THE SECRETS OF THE RUNES

Something the runes have that our letters definitely don't have is inherent meaning. To review, each rune has a meaning associated with it, not to be confused with the meaning of its name. The meaning of the name is usually quite simple and often illustrative. If you think of the children's alphabet books we have nowadays that pair each letter with a well-known object, i.e. "F is for Fox, G is for Goat", etc., the name meanings were a bit like that. (McCoy, n.d.h) We could even imagine our own Futhark picture book. It would start "ᚠ is for fehu", accompanied by a picture of cows.

The meaning of the rune itself is more a concept or a quality. It would be harder to explain to children or illustrate with a simple picture. However, you will often find that there is a connection between the name meaning and the rune meaning. Below, I'll examine each of the meanings and those connections. (As with the name meanings, the rune meanings are taken from the website Norse Mythology for Smart People, which has handily collected all the information on the Elder Futhark from the rune poems, in particular the Old English Rune Poem.) The observations on the connections between name meanings and rune meanings are generally my own, though.

ᚠ

The ᚠ (fehu) rune has a meaning of wealth. This could be money or other material riches. Consider the name meaning - "cattle." In medieval society, ownership of cattle was a significant measure of wealth. So think of this rune not just as indicating zeros at the end of a bank account balance, but also other measures of wealth such as communal status and property possession.

ᚢ

The rune ᚢ (uruz) indicates determination and conviction. Remember that this rune's name means "aurochs", a kind of wild oxen. The phrase "stubborn as an ox" comes to mind, doesn't it? This rune is about a kind of mental strength that is able to carry you through something from sheer force of will.

ᚦ

The ᚦ (thurisaz) rune is an unhappy one, or at least an

ominous one. It means peril or pain. The name meaning for this rune is "giant", and so you can see that this rune is associated with the darker parts of life. It is not all negative, though. Remember that the giants and their dark world are considered a part of the natural order, and there are even some pagans who venerate or otherwise work with the jötnar.

ᚠ

In opposition to the previous rune, the ᚠ (ansuz) rune is about flourishing and thriving. This makes sense, when you remember that the name of the rune points to the Aesir gods. While the þ rune invokes the qualities of the jötnar, the ᚠ rune invokes the orderly prosperity of the gods of Asgard.

ᚱ

The rune ᚱ (raidho) is about moving forward. Its name means a journey taken on a horse, which would suggest both power and momentum. It can mean movement in both a psychological way, such as personal growth, and in a more concrete way, such as a career move or another big life change.

ᚲ

The ᚲ (kaunan) rune, like the þ rune, also means pain. Its name meaning, however, is "ulcer", which suggests a more physically located pain than the chaotic eternal darkness that the jötnar might make you contemplate. In keeping with that interpretation, this rune is also said to represent mortality.

ᚷ

You can see from the chart above that the name of ᚷ (gebo)

means "gift", and its rune meaning is almost identical. It means generosity, and like the idea of gifts, generosity can be found in a number of ways - not just things given, but also time, effort, and even other abstract ideas like mercy or magnanimity.

ᛈ

The ᛈ (wunjo) rune has perhaps the most straightforward meaning, and it also has the most similar name and rune meaning - by which I mean both are exactly the same. The name and the rune itself both mean "joy." This is not just happiness, but an exciting kind of joy, almost to the point of being overwhelmed.

ᚺ

Like the runes ᚠ and ᚦ, it seems that ᛈ and ᚺ could form a pair. Where ᛈ means joy, ᚺ (hagalaz) means chaos or destruction. However, while ᛈ has the same name and rune meaning, the name meaning for ᚺ is hail - the hard, icy precipitation that though small can cause great damage. Hail can also form quite suddenly, developing out of rain when the temperature drops. The linking of ᚺ to this specific kind of wild and damaging weather shows that this force is something to be reckoned with.

ᚾ

The ᚾ (naudhiz) rune is another one where the name and rune meanings align almost completely. Both the name and rune can mean "need"; the rune can also be taken to mean not a need in the form of something necessary, but an emotional need (what we might call a "want") which has gone unrealized.

ᛋ

The name meaning for ᛃ (jera) is "year", so it makes sense that the rune meaning is "harvest." The harvest was a major festival for most medieval societies, who relied on the food they would reap to get them through the winter, and it was a high point in the yearly cycle of seasons. The ᛃ rune also has the additional meaning of "reward", which makes sense as well. When you have planted and tended something until it has grown to fruition, reaping what you've grown is a reward for your hard work.

ᛇ

The ᛇ (eihwaz) rune can mean stability or strength. Remember its name meaning is yew, as in the yew tree. In the middle ages, the yew tree was prized for its wood, which was used in weapons. Yews also live for a long time, and were believed to have protective powers that ward off evil. (Barth, n.d.) Yew is also one of the possible species for the world tree. So there are many layers to the meaning represented by this rune.

ᛉ

The ᛉ rune has a slightly more complex meaning than many of its fellow runes. It means defense or protection, but specifically, defense of someone or something that is beloved, and protection from foes (as opposed to, say, natural disasters or bad luck). This rune is an interesting case because while the meaning is known, the meaning of the name is not. It is the only rune in the Elder Futhark where this is the case.

ᛋ

The ᛋ (sowilo) rune's name meaning is the sun, and perhaps symbolized the light of the sun shining upon you not just literally but metaphorically as well, because the rune has two positive meanings: success and comfort.

↑

While the ⧢ rune means success, the ↑ (Tiwaz) rune means victory. It can also mean honor, which makes sense, considering the strong association in early Norse culture and Nore mythology of honor with warriors and victory in battle. The ↑ rune's name represents the god Tiwaz, which is an earlier version of the god Tyr. As we learned in chapter two, Tyr is a god of warriors and victory.

ß

The ß (berkanan) rune, like the ᚱ rune, represents growth. But rather than the sort of powerful forward momentum that ᚱ suggests, the kind of ß invokes is one connected to nature and the growing of plants, food, and other life (including procreation). Fittingly, the name meaning is birch, a tree that was sacred to Freyja, goddess of fertility. (Woolf, 2016)

ᛗ

The rune ᛗ (ehwaz) has a very sweet meaning. It represents companionship and the positive traits that mark good relationships, such as faith and trust. The name meaning for the ᛗ rune is horse, which suggests that while we think of dogs as man's best friend, the ancient Norse probably would have suggested a horse, instead.

ᛗ

The ᛗ (mannaz) rune is the other piece of the horse-man

companionship - the man. Its name meaning is man, and its rune meaning can be enhancement or support. I think the best interpretation of the meaning is one that encompasses both - the idea of not just man but mankind, working together to support one another in a way that enhances the world we all create together.

ᛚ

Moving back into the darker side of life's balance, the ᛚ (laguz) rune is all about disorder. Just as with þ, however, that's not necessarily a negative thing. Just as darkness has a place in Norse magic, so too does the unknown and the yet-to-be. Like Ginnungagap, the void at the beginning of the world, there is potential in the darkness, the chaotic, and the formless - and that's what this rune represents.

◇

After potential comes realization, which is what the next rune ◇ (Ingwaz) represents. Like Tiwaz, Ingwaz is the early name of a god with a much more common name - in this case, Freyr. As discussed in chapter two, Freyr was associated with the sun and fruitfulness, so it makes sense that this rune, meaning germination, the start of something, or the manifestation of possibility, would be given his name.

ᛟ

The name meaning for the ᛟ (othalan) rune is inheritance, and the rune itself also has that meaning. Along with inheritance, this rune can also mean other ideas related to heritage, such as customs or tradition, and noble birth.

ᛗ

The last of the Elder Futhark runes, ᛞ (dagaz) ends things on a bright note. Just as its name meaning, "day", represents the coming of physical light, this rune represents metaphorical light, meaning happiness and hope.

ᛁ & ᛤ

You may have noticed that I didn't include the ᛁ (isaz) or ᛤ runes above. This is because the meanings for these runes are unknown. And as you can see from my omission in the prior sentence, the name of the ᛤ rune is also unknown.

A note about rune symbolism in the wider world: Just like some of the symbols discussed in chapter six, some runes have been appropriated by white nationalist groups or their members. Many modern Norse pagans are fighting to remove these associations and reclaim the runes for their original meanings.

Hopefully you've found the history of the runes through the centuries as fascinating as I find it. I really loved writing this chapter and giving you some insight into how they were developed, how they were used, and how they've changed. I also enjoyed getting into a little more detail about the Elder Futhark, introducing you to all the letters in that futhark, their names, and their meanings. In the next chapter, we're going to get into how to do magic with these runes. I'm excited to show you - let's go!

CHAPTER 8

CARVINGS OF FATE

There is a quote from author Margaret Atwood that always comes to mind when I'm thinking about rune magic: "A word after a word after a word is power." She was referring, of course, to her profession and the novels she wrote, but it always struck me as the perfect way to describe the relationship of early Norse people with runes. Nowadays we often use words very casually, but early civilizations had a reverence and even a healthy fear of the power of words. They recognized something that we would also do well to remember, which is that words do not just communicate and describe, they can also sway and create.

Perhaps one of the most compelling, and harrowing, images in all of Norse mythology is that of Odin hanging himself on the world tree in order to gain knowledge of the runes. Whatever their historical background, however they came to be the runes we know and use today, there is no separating them from this story of pain and endurance. Whether taken as legend or metaphor, the story of Odin's sacrifice is the perfect entry point for learning rune magic, because it tells us the most important thing - that the power of the runes is precious, and we should wield it and respect it accordingly.

Runes were associated not just with Yggdrasil but with the well beneath it where the norns dwelled. The poem Völuspá suggests that the norns carved fates into the world tree, and some believe this is a reference to the creation of the runes. (McCoy, n.d.g) This association of wyrd (fate) with the runes is another clue to how runes were viewed in ancient times, and how we should approach them today. To work with rune magic requires you not to think of runes as mechanical signifiers but as intrinsic pieces of our world and the web of fate that connects us all.

Remember our discussion of phonosemantic theory, and the idea that all parts of the rune (look, sound, name) carry meaning? This also implies that runes have an intrinsic meaning that exists outside of traditional language. This quality may very well be part of where runes get their power - their inherent meaning is so embedded in the quality of their existence, it can be felt even by those who do not speak the same language. (McCoy, n.d.g) This will be a point of contention among scholars and pagans alike - some will argue that it is our use of runes that make them magical, and others will argue that the runes themselves have inherent magical qualities. I offer you both opinions, because it's the sort of discussion which will never be closed, and I think it's best that people decide for themselves what they think about it.

However, choosing one side or the other of that debate is not crucial to using runic magic. You can believe that the runes are a system created for communication which has over the centuries been incorporated into a plethora of magical practices, or you can believe runes from their very creation were symbols of great and mysterious power. Either way, your approach should be the same. Respect the power that the runes have, wherever it comes from, and know that knowledge and hard work are the two things that will pay off the most in your own runic spells.

THE WAYS OF RUNES

Most present-day methods for using runes cannot be traced all the way back to pagan Scandinavia. Instead, they are a combination of what we know about that early world and magical practices from later periods. (Knightly, n.d.m) As mentioned in the last chapter, people like Guido von List and Ralph Blum influenced a great deal of modern rune magic. Guido von List claimed to have been given a vision of a previously unknown set of runes that pre-dated all the other runic systems - however, he also linked his idea on rune magic to his own racism, and much of his ideas have therefore been discarded. There was another surge of interest in runes in the 1980s, which is when Ralph Blum's Book of Runes was published. This book would go on to influence many of the books on runes that would come after it. (Grimfrost, 2017)

So our modern practice is a product of centuries of non-Norse influence, and the exact nature of runic magic in the middle ages and earlier is, like so much of the early Norse religion, a bit of a mystery. However, the common belief that runes held power and that power could be wielded through the carving and writing of these runes is attested to by many sources, including not only the Eddas and the sagas, but also the writings of Tacitus all the way back in first century CE. Tacitus observed rune magic being used to cast lots, a form of divination. I should note that he does not describe the exact runes being used, so we do not know for certain whether he observed the same Norse runes we know today. (Folmer, 2016) Additionally, the Romans observed tribes from further north casting sticks with runes carved onto them, and the Poetic Edda has a Valkyrie character who gives a speech about rune magic. (Grimfrost, 2017)

Archeologists have also discovered physical evidence for runic magic in the form of objects inscribed with runes that were surmised to be talismans. What none of these things can give us is instructions on how runic magic was actually practiced, because these were passed down orally, and also almost certainly varied from place to place. (Folmer, 2016) It's a good thing, then, that we are working within a tradition that allows for multiple meanings and people to find their own way. But as Norse paganism is also a tradition of wisdom, I'll use the rest of this chapter to give you an overview of basic rune magic, so you can hopefully feel empowered to start your own practices.

FORM, SOUND, AND MEANING

When most people talk about runes, they are probably referring to what's called the rune's "form" - the visual symbol that is drawn to represent the rune. One interesting thing about rune forms is that they never involve horizontal lines - only diagonal and vertical lines. (Leìt, 2020) As an exercise to help strengthen your connection to the runes, you can practice visualizing their forms. Start with a very plain idea of a rune - if you like, you can print the rune on a piece of paper and spend time looking at it. Then you want to close your eyes and be able to see the rune clearly with your mind's eye. Once you are able to do this with plain runes, you can add other details, such as colors or textures. With every layer of complexity, you become more connected to the rune, and better able to invoke its power. (Leìt, 2020)

The form of a rune is actually only one-third of its existence, however. The second part of a rune is its sound. As I mentioned in chapter four, the term galdr is believed to refer to a kind of magic that uses incantations and runes. (McCoy, n.d.d) Galdr refers to the speaking of incantations, but it naturally goes with runes because the sound of runes is as important as their form. Galdr can be something as complex as a fully composed song, or as simple as chanting the name of one rune over and over again. You can also "chant" a rune's form by writing it repeatedly. Not only can this sort of chanting help you to focus on your objective and conjure the rune's power, it can also deepen your connection with the rune. (Leìt, 2020) If you are looking to strengthen your rune magic even further, you can also combine the practices of visualizing and chanting.

The final part of a rune is its meaning. We've already discussed the meanings of the Elder Futhark runes in the previous chapter. These meanings are the wisdom that gives weight to the sight and sound of a rune. You might focus on the rune's form and sound while you are performing a spell or working to train your mind, but the meaning of the rune will be what you use when you choose which runes will work for which spells, or when interpreting the results of a rune casting.

Another thing to consider both when you are inscribing and casting runes is the rune's positions. There are three ways a rune can be positioned: direct (as they've been presented so far in this book), inverted or reversed (just as it sounds, the rune is turned upside down), and mirrored. The most interesting of these to me is mirrored, as there are some runes that have no mirrored version, and some runes that are actually mirrored versions of other runes. The runes | and ᛝ do not have mirrored versions. Meanwhile, ᛈ is ᚦ mirrored, ᛘ is ᚠ mirrored, and ◇ is ᚲ mirrored. Mirrored runes can sometimes be used just for embellishment, but they are also common in bindrunes. The doubling of a rune's form that occurs when that rune is mirrored strengthens the power or effect of that rune. (Leìt, 2020)

A SIMPLE RUNE SPELL

The earliest practitioners of rune magic were the völur, who were known for their powers of prophecy. The völur were so good at their jobs they were even consulted by the gods from time to time. There are some "modern-day" völur who dedicate their professional lives to learning to read the runes and use them in magical practice. However, there are plenty of people who incorporate rune magic into their lives in much smaller ways. (Leìt, 2020)

The most basic type of rune magic is done by adding runes to significant objects in your life. This can be things that you wear or objects in your home, or anything else that you can think of - the limit is your own innovation. There is no "proper" procedure for creating something like this, but if you like you can time its creation with a particular day, season, phase of the moon, or other significant moment. The one thing you should be sure to do is to focus on what you want the rune to do for you as you are inscribing it. You want to be able to channel your energy into the object and the runic inscription. (Brethauer, n.d.) You can make this inscription out of one rune, out of a line of runes, or even out of bindrunes.

When using runes for amulets and other magic that involves imbuing objects with the rune's power, the last step is to activate the rune. There's a good deal of overlap in activating runes and charging other magical objects, such as crystals. However, activating a rune starts with ruminating on the purpose of the rune - think of what you hope it will bring you, and get as specific as you can. After this, some people like to wrap the object and keep it somewhere dark to let the energy "steep." Once you feel enough time has passed, you can take the rune out and charge it. You can do this in whatever way you like. Some common methods are with your own breath, with oils or incense, with moonlight, or even with a combination of some or all of these. Remember that this sort of thing is a kind of spell, and once you've completed it, you should close it as you would any ritual. (Brethauer, n.d.)

The practice of activation is one way that the magical use of runes is distinguished from the many other ways that they are and have been used. It also protects the magic a bit, as it requires you not to just write or say a combination of runes, but rather to genuinely understand the runes and put something of yourself into their activation before you will see results. (Leìt, 2020) During both the inscription and activation rituals, you can invoke a deity (or multiple deities, if you choose). You can ask your deity to guide your choices and to help you achieve the purpose of the inscription. If you do so, be sure to give them a small offering. It is also polite to give an offering to your deity after the rune has accomplished its intended task.

BINDRUNES - NOT JUST FOR BLUETOOTH

Bindrune magic involves combining runes together with attention paid to the runes' meanings, in order to create a specific magical effect. (Do not confuse bindrunes with galdrastafur - they have similar aesthetics but very different processes.) (Knightly, n.d.m) Early bindrunes probably were more about depicting names or adding a decorative touch to a runic inscription, but by the late middle ages they were being used for magical purposes. You can combine runes in any way you like when making a bindrune; they don't have to be kept in any certain position. The best combination is one that speaks to you, as it will be your energy that is creating the power of the symbol. (Brethauer, n.d.)

However, there are different categories of bindrunes based on the way the runes are put together. Linear stacked bindrunes layer two runes in the same space, lining up their centers. (Very rarely, three runes will be combined in this way.) Linear same-stave bindrunes place multiple runes in a row, either vertically or horizontally. Radial bindrunes place multiple runes around a central point. These are also sometimes called staves, and a similar configuration is used in Galdrastafir as well. You can use the categories of bindrunes in whichever way you see fit, but it is common to use linear stacked runes to conjure, linear same-stave bindrunes to address obstacles, and radial bindrunes to protect. (Time Nomads, 2021a)

To make your own bindrune, first be sure you have spent sufficient time studying the runes themselves. I don't recommend starting with bindrunes before you're spent time working with the runes on an individual basis. This will help you not only to know the runes well, but also to gain an understanding of how the runes work with you, in particular. Again, rune magic is a meeting of the rune's energy with your own - don't discount that fact!

Once you feel you're ready to create a bindrune, the process is actually quite simple. You decide your goal, decide which runes will help you achieve it, and decide how you will put them together. It's fine to sketch ideas of different configurations - this can actually help you to consider many possibilities, and choose the one that feels strongest and most connected to you and your goal. Once you have selected a design, then you'll inscribe it on your chosen object. You'll want this object to be something that you will interact with regularly, such as something you can wear, or something that will hang in a place where you'll see it daily. (Time Nomads, 2021a) As with any other runic inscription, approach the creation of the bindrune with focus and intention.

RIST YOUR OWN RUNES

Making your own runes, also called "risting", is something of a rite of passage for those who are serious about rune magic. You can make runes however you please, but traditionally they are made from wood, preferably the wood of a tree that grows nuts or fruit. Some people choose to leave the wood of their rune set raw, while others opt for a reddish stain, purportedly invoking the blood that might have been used to mark such sacred items in earlier times. The most important thing to remember is that you are making the runes to be used for a hallowed purpose, so you should approach the task earnestly, and not before you've studied the subject. (Wigington, 2019c)

Other options for rune materials include stones or baked clay. Some rune sets are made of bone, which can be off-putting to some people, but appealing to others. It is recommended bone sets only be made from bones of animals that died of natural causes. Whatever material you choose, make sure the pieces are small enough that you can easily hold them all in your hands. This will be important for casting. (Time Nomads, 2021b) Just as with inscribing runes on other objects, the time you spend creating your rune set should be a time when you're able to focus on the runes and deepen your connection with them.

In addition to the runes of the Elder Futhark, a 25th rune will sometimes be added to rune sets. This rune is not actually a rune at all, but a blank space - a piece of the same size and shape as the rest of your runes, but with nothing written on it. This is called "Odin's rune" or "the wyrd rune." (Time Nomads, 2021b) Whether you make your rune set or purchase one, you can bless it to prepare it for use and make it feel more like it belongs to you. You can use any method you like; elemental blessings like fire, water, or air (incense) are popular and work very well.

In addition to amulets and bindrunes, one of the most common types of rune magic - perhaps the most common type of rune magic - is rune casting. This is a form of divination where runes are drawn and interpreted to answer questions about the future or offer guidance on issues that you might be facing. Because divination within the Norse pagan tradition is so closely associated with rune casting, I will talk about both of those things in the next chapter.

CHAPTER 9
CASTING THE FUTURE

There have been many, many books and films and other stories whose plots revolved around seeing into the future. The ability to predict what will happen next is a common power for characters in science fiction and fantasy - and understandably so. Who wouldn't want to know what will happen tomorrow, next year, in ten years? It's a very tempting idea, even if many of those same stories also attempt to show us the inevitable downsides of such a power. Often these fictional characters are plagued by misinterpretations, or anxiety at knowing what bad things are coming, while also being powerless to stop it.

You don't have to worry about those downsides with the kind of divination I'm about to teach you. That kind of "superhero" idea of divination, as a power that suddenly gives you visions that tell you exactly what the future will be, is quite different from the sort of divination we'll discuss in this chapter. Divination in Norse magic is about looking to the future not to change it, but to understand how you can integrate your destiny into a life that you'll find fulfilling. (McCoy, n.d.d) It isn't about predicting the lottery numbers or seeing the face of your soulmate. It's about giving yourself the wisdom you need to guide your own actions, and creating the best life for yourself. It goes back to the idea of the web of wyrd. The future is a reality that we are all creating now, that we are weaving out of our present actions.

SEIDR AND DIVINATION - MAGIC WANDS AND SPECIAL SEATS

I've mentioned the völur at a few points now in the books. While they practiced different forms of magical arts, the völur were best known as seers. The singular of völur, völva, is generally understood to mean a "seeress." There is a poem told by a völva in the Poetic Edda that explains how the universe was created and how it would end. This poem is called the Völuspá, and it is where we get the most detailed description of Ragnarok, the end of the world. (Manea, 2021) The Völuspá is begun by Odin himself, in yet another of his quests for knowledge. He gives jewelry to the völva in exchange for the history she knows and the future she foretells. (NMD, n.d.h) This is the most famous reference to völur and their prophecies in early Norse society, but it is far from the only one.

Another famous mention of a völva is found in the story of Erik the Red, a well-known Viking saga that you might have learned about in elementary school when your class studied the Vikings. (McCoy, n.d.j) There is also archeological evidence for the existence of the völur, most prominently the discovery of the type of wands they were known to use in graves alongside female bodies (and occasionally males, as well). From the Eddas and sagas, we know that völva traveled from place to place and were always well-received because of the help that they would bring wherever they went. (NMD, n.d.h)

The völur were closely associated with the practice of seidr. In fact, it's possible that the word "seidr" comes from the same root word as "seat", in reference to the place where the völva sat whilst undertaking their spiritual journeys. (VAL, n.d.) We briefly discussed seidr in chapter four. This type of magic, which involved entering a trance and leaving one's body, has been compared to types of shamanism from other parts of the world. Specifically, there are potential links between the practice of seidr and the shamans of the Saami people who lived in the northernmost parts of Scandinavia. (VAL, n.d.) The norns, Odin, and Freyja were all known to practice seidr. It was thought to be a powerful magic, one that made the völur feared at times. While seidr was seen as a female act in an extremely gendered society, Odin was not alone in his practice, as there are quite a few records of men who learned these magical arts. (McCoy, n.d.j)

As I just mentioned, völur were known to work with wands and to own specially-made chairs that, when sat upon, allowed the völvur's spirits to move beyond their body. Sound was also an element in the völur's practices, as they would recruit girls to sit around them and chant or sing in order to help them enter the right state of mind to access their powers. While the most common requests had to do with divination, it was also believed that a völva could influence the physical world, strengthening friends and weakening foes. (NMD, n.d.h) The idea of the völur being able to influence the world may seem unrelated to the ability to tell the future, but when you remember the web of wyrd and the way all life is connected, you start to see how the ability to view the threads of the web and the ability to tug on them are no so far apart.

Other terms for those who worked seidr magic were seid-kona or spá-kona (kona loosely translates to wife, so you can see even in the language the assumption that the practitioner would be female). The term spá-kona was often used by women who wanted to avoid the association with what was perceived as the darker parts of seidr powers. The "spá" in spá-kona designates an ability to see or manipulate orlog. There was also the title "heidr", which is related to the word heathen and means another type of female magic practitioner, sometimes translated as "witch." (VAL, n.d.)

Of course, with the liberal use of the word witch by the Christian authorities, who applied it to any type of perceived magical power that was not in the hands of their male clergy, many different categories of magic workers could be placed under the umbrella of the word witch. And unfortunately, while other elements of Norse paganism survived and blended into the new Christian world of the late medieval period, the völva were cast as evil forces in the eyes of Christendom, and many völva were accused of destructive witchcraft. Those that did survive were forced to hide their magical ways. (NMD, n.d.h)

HOW TO CAST RUNES

As mentioned in the last chapter, in the first century the Roman historian Tacitus described Germanic tribes casting lots using pieces of wood with writing on them. He talks about how the branches were cut and inscribed with markings (presumably runes) and then thrown onto a white cloth. Three pieces of wood are then selected, and their meaning interpreted. (Hopkins & Downing, 2017) Amazing, this is a pretty accurate description of how you will cast runes. Our modern method of rune casting remains largely the same as it was even back in the first century.

Just a reminder before we get started: Casting runes is not about predicting what will happen in the future. Rather, it's about finding answers to questions you have, perhaps questions about decisions you have to make, or about the direction of a relationship. Casting works best if you have a specific question in your mind, something that you can focus on, so that the casting will also have focus. The ideal questions for a divination session will be specific but open-ended. You don't want to ask about general things, as the answers you get might be equally vague. However, you want to leave space for the runes to give you more complex answers than you might have been anticipating. Recording the runes you cast so that you can review them later is a good idea. (Brethauer, n.d.)

Runes help us to clarify which direction we are going, and how our lives might change if we change directions. (Wigington, 2019c) So it is helpful to think of it as looking for your own path through the world, rather than looking for a map of what happens next. This applies not just to the questions you seek to answer, but also to the way you interpret the runes you cast. The process of interpreting runes is not prescriptive. Yes, each rune has a meaning, but those meanings can be interpreted in many, many ways. Getting to know the runes is a big part of using them in divination, as the greater your connection to the runes, the better you will be able to receive and interpret the wisdom they have for you. (Brethauer, n.d.) Don't get stuck on one idea of a meaning, and miss the other possible ways that a rune might be interpreted. And trust your own intuition if you're trying to decide between two interpretations.

You can technically cast on any surface, but it is traditional to lay out a white square of fabric to throw the runes on. The reasoning behind the fabric is to create a space that is sacred to the casting, much like a circle is made for many pagan spells. (Wigington, 2020) For some people, this is very important. Others may choose to cast on their altar, or on the ground, or on some other space that they've consecrated. Remember not to rush the process. Your connection to the runes and your state of mind is paramount. In the same way that the first step of performing a blót is to enter the right state of mind, the first step of casting is to clear your mind and then focus on what it is that you are hoping to discover.

You can start simply with a three-rune cast. Throw the runes (gently!) onto your casting space. One important thing is to never look at the runes as you cast them. Continue not to look as you select three runes. Alternatively, some people will shuffle their runes in a bag or other container, and then draw out three and place them on the white cloth. (Wigington, 2020) These three runes are the runes meant to answer your question. You want to think about what they mean by themselves, and also what they might mean in combination.

Some people believe there is one rune each for the past, present, and future. You can decide for yourself if you'd like to use this method of interpretation - perhaps sometimes you will and sometimes you won't, depending on what sort of question you are asking. (Brethauer, n.d.) Another common framework for a three-rune cast is for the first rune to represent the broad picture, the second to home in on the problem at hand, and the third to offer solutions. (Wigington, 2020) I think either of these ways can work; you don't have to use either. Whatever you choose, however, I recommend making the choice before you cast. This allows the runes to work with you, and it also prevents you from picking and choosing among various interpretation methods to find the one that tells you what you want to hear.

Once you start to feel comfortable with casting and reading three runes, you can start casting with more than three. Another common number is nine, for its significance in Norse mythology. The more runes you cast, the more complex your casting and its interpretation can become. You can start looking at the positions of the runes, and how they are laying. A general rule of thumb is the runes that are closer to the center of your casting area and the ones that land face up are the most important ones to focus on. (Wigington, 2020)

If runes are reversed, this can be taken as cautionary or pointing to some deficiency. This does not mean the rune has the "opposite" meaning. Rather, it indicates that you should look for vulnerability or be aware of how you are lacking in a quality. For example, a reverse ᚢ (uruz) rune may be telling you that your current issues are being caused by a lack of conviction or willpower.

You should always pay attention to the whole reading, but repeated runes will usually be paramount, as it is a message that is important enough to be given to you multiple times. You should always keep your mind open so that you won't miss important information just because you're not expecting it. In particular, pay attention to any runes that you don't think make sense. Sit with those runes and consider how they might offer answers. (Brethauer, n.d.) Think outside the box.

DIVINATION BEYOND THE RUNES

You can also do an extremely rudimentary casting without ready-made runes, if you have sticks, twigs, or other small, straight objects. Throw these and then see if you can make out any runes in the patterns that form. (Brethauer, n.d.) This is obviously a much less precise method of divination, and can be tricky as our minds tend to want to find patterns even when none exist. However, it can sometimes be helpful if you're struggling with other methods. At the very least, it will tell you what sort of runes your mind is hoping - or dreading - to see.

Another way to predict the future that was common in the middle ages was omens. Usually omens were connected to nature. They could be found in the appearance of an animal or group of animals, or with the occurrence of specific types of weather. (NMD, n.d.f) Omens were also known as auspices, and they are mentioned along with casting in the account of the Roman Tacitus. Omens were often sought after a casting was made, in hopes that the two forms of divination would align, giving definite guidance to those seeking it. (Hopkins & Downing, 2017)

In modern practice, omens can be much subtler. We've already discussed omens as signs from your chosen deity. There is no rule or definitive way to determine what counts as an omen. The only person who can truly decide if you've been given an omen is you, so pay attention to your own feelings on the matter, as well as how likely the omen was to have been coincidental, and whether or not the omen is telling you something you want to hear, versus something you might not want - but need - to hear. And once again, you can apply the rule of three, where you look for three signs in a row as confirmation that the message is not coincidence or your own bias. (Knightly, n.d.b)

It is not unheard of for Norse pagans to also incorporate other methods of divination, which are not specifically Norse, into their practice. This is absolutely fine if you feel led to do so. Just as it is acceptable for Norse pagans to have poly-affiliations that include deities outside Norse mythology, it is acceptable to include other pagan practices into your magic. The only thing that is not acceptable is to include a practice without understanding it or taking the time to perform it correctly.

FINAL WORDS

Sadly now, friends, we've come to the end of our time together. I've worked hard to put this book together as a beginner's guide to Norse magic, and if you've read the entire book, you've also worked hard. Well done!

It may seem like a long time ago that we started by discussing the influence of Norse magic on our world today, and I promised to be your humble docent in your journey getting to know more about the past and present of that influence. Now that you've finished this book, you know the history of medieval Norse culture, where much of Norse paganism and magic started, and how those practices led to the Norse pagan traditions of the modern world.

From this, you've also gained an understanding of the philosophy behind Norse paganism, and you know about the major gods and goddesses of Norse mythology, as well as key figures like the norns, the jötnar, and the world tree. You learned about the nine noble virtues; you know what frith, wyrd, orlog, and blöts are; you have a basic understanding of the Norse pagan calendar and are familiar with the most prominent symbols from Norse history, mythology, and religion.

And you have all you need to know to begin a practice of Norse magic, including how to perform rituals, how to use runes in your spells, and how to cast runes for guidance on the future.

I hope you're proud of yourself - that was a lot to learn! And don't worry if you're not sure you remember it all. Learning is a lifelong pursuit, as Odin himself taught us. You can go back at any time and read through this book again.

I do hope there are two things that have stuck with you, though. The first is that there is power here for the taking - power in the runes, power in the rituals, and power in your own connection to the world, to the divine, and to the web of wyrd that connects us all. And the second is that you are responsible for your own path through the realm of Norse magic. This means that the onus is on you to put in the work, to study and to practice. But it also means that you can shape your life and your magical practice how you like.

I've given you the beginnings of knowledge and skills that you can build upon to make something that is truly your own. I hope the end of this book is just the beginning of your journey. I wish you well, and will leave you with two runes of growth: the ᚱ rune to speed you on your journey, and the ᛒ to help you be fruitful and bloom in your practice.

REFERENCES

Anti-Defamation League. (n.d.a) "Thor's Hammer." ADL.org. Accessed January 23rd, 2022. https://www.adl.org/education/references/hate-symbols/thors-hammer

Anti-Defamation League. (n.d.b) "Valknot." ADL.org. Accessed January 23rd, 2022. https://www.adl.org/education/references/hate-symbols/valknot

The Asatru Community. (n.d.) "What is a Blot?" TheAsatruCommunity.org. Accessed January 24th, 2022. https://www.theasatrucommunity.org/blot

Atkins, Harry. (2018, June 5). "The Hidden Meanings Behind Viking Runes." HistoryHit.com. Accessed January 29th, 2022. https://www.historyhit.com/the-hidden-meanings-behind-viking-runes/

Barth, Brian. (n.d.) "Yew Trees." LovetoKnow.com. Accessed January 30th, 2022. https://garden.lovetoknow.com/wiki/Yew

BBC. (2003, October 30). "Heathenry." BBC Online. Accessed January 19th, 2022. https://www.bbc.co.uk/religion/religions/paganism/subdivisions/heathenry_1.shtml

Berloga Workshop. (2019, June 23). "Valknut: the Norse Mystery." Berloga-Workshop.com. Accessed January 23rd, 2022. https://berloga-workshop.com/blog/28-valknut-the-norse-mystery.html

Brethauer, Amanda. (n.d.) "Norse Runes, Viking Symbols, and How To Use These Magic Runes in 2021." ThePeculiarBrunette.com. Accessed January 30th, 2022. https://www.thepeculiarbrunette.com/rune-symbols-meanings-and-uses/

Britannica, T. Editors of Encyclopaedia. (1998, July 20). "Yggdrasill." Encyclopedia Britannica. Accessed January 14th, 2022. https://www.britannica.com/topic/Yggdrasill

Eds., Symbolsage. (n.d.) "Vegvisir Symbol - Origins and History." Symbolsage.com. Accessed January 24th, 2022. https://symbolsage.com/vegvisir-symbol-origins-and-history/

Folmer, Xander. (2016, March 23). "Ranting Recon: Does Magic Have Any Place in Heathenry?" HeathenHof.com. Accessed January 22, 2022. http://www.heathenhof.com/ranting-recon-does-magic-have-any-place-in-heathenry/

Grimfrost. (2017, September 11). "Carving Runes." Grimfrost.com. Accessed January 30th, 2022. https://grimfrost.com/blogs/blog/carving-runes

Härger, Arith. (2016, November 18). "How to Blot? - The Basics." Whispers of Yggdrasil. Accessed January 24th, 2022. https://arithharger.wordpress.com/2016/11/18/how-to-blot-the-basics/

Harper, Douglas. (n.d.). "Etymology of orthopraxy." Online Etymology Dictionary. Accessed January 21, 2022. https://www.etymonline.com/word/orthopraxy

Helgason, Magnús Sveinn. (2015, August 7). "Visit the only heathen temple in Iceland in Skagafjörður fjord for a pagan grill party this Saturday." Iceland Magazine. Accessed January 17th, 2022. https://web.archive.org/web/20151008121439/http://icelandmag.visir.is/tags/asheimar

Hogarth, Samuel. "Vegvisir in Norse Mythology." Reykjavikcars.com. Accessed January 24th, 2022. https://www.reykjavikcars.com/blog/icelandic-culture/vegvisir-symbol-meaning

Hopkins, Joseph & Ross Downing. (2017, March 12). "Godshapes I: Hœnir, Bird-God?" Mimisbrunnr.Info. Accessed January 30th, 2022. https://www.mimisbrunnr.info/news/2017/2/6/godshapes-i-hnir-bird-god

Knightly, Zander Hjörvard. (n.d.a) "Creation." Skald's Keep. Accessed January 13th, 2022. https://skaldskeep.com/norse/creation/

Knightly, Zander Hjörvard. (n.d.b) "Deity & Spirit Work 101." Skald's Keep. Accessed January 13th, 2022. https://skaldskeep.com/deity-and-spirit-work-101/

Knightly, Zander Hjörvard. (n.d.c) "Developing a Norse Pagan Practice." Skald's Keep. Accessed January 13th, 2022. https://skaldskeep.com/norse/practice/

Knightly, Zander Hjörvard. (n.d.d) "Frith & Hospitality." Skald's Keep. Accessed January 13th, 2022. https://skaldskeep.com/norse/frith-hospitality/

Knightly, Zander Hjörvard. (n.d.e) "The Gifting Cycle." Skald's Keep. Accessed January 13th, 2022. https://skaldskeep.com/norse/gifting-cycle/

Knightly, Zander Hjörvard. (n.d.f) "The History of Norse Paganism." Skald's Keep. Accessed January 13th, 2022. https://skaldskeep.com/norse/history/

Knightly, Zander Hjörvard. (n.d.g) "Intro to Norse Paganism." Skald's Keep. Accessed January 13th, 2022. https://skaldskeep.com/norse/intro/

Knightly, Zander Hjörvard. (n.d.h) "Morality & Ethics." Skald's Keep. Accessed January 13th, 2022. https://skaldskeep.com/norse/morality/

Knightly, Zander Hjörvard. (n.d.i) "Norse Pagan Holidays." Skald's Keep. Accessed January 13th, 2022. https://skaldskeep.com/norse/holidays/

Knightly, Zander Hjörvard. (n.d.j) "Norse Pagan Magic." Skald's Keep. Accessed January 13th, 2022. https://skaldskeep.com/norse/magic/

Knightly, Zander Hjörvard. (n.d.k) "Norse Pagan Practice Formats." Skald's Keep. Accessed January 13th, 2022. https://skaldskeep.com/norse/formats/

Knightly, Zander Hjörvard. (n.d.l) "Rituals." Skald's Keep. Accessed January 13th, 2022. https://skaldskeep.com/norse/rituals/

Knightly, Zander Hjörvard. (n.d.m) "Runes." Skald's Keep.

Accessed January 13th, 2022. https://skaldskeep.com/
norse/runes/

Knightly, Zander Hjörvard. (n.d.n) "Veneration." Skald's Keep.
Accessed January 13th, 2022. https://skaldskeep.com/
norse/veneration/

Knightly, Zander Hjörvard. (n.d.o) "Wyrd & Orlog." Skald's Keep.
Accessed January 13th, 2022. https://skaldskeep.com/
norse/wyrd/

Knightly, Zander Hjörvard. (n.d.p) "Yggdrasil." Skald's Keep.
Accessed January 13th, 2022. https://skaldskeep.com/
norse/yggdrasil/

Kornevall, Andreas. (2021, January 5). "Norse Ceremony - The
Blot." Kornevall.com. Accessed January 24th, 2022. https://www.
kornevall.com/post/norse-ceremonial-architecture-blot

Leìt. (2020, June 26). "Runic Magic - History and Practice."
LunarSpell.com. Accessed January 30th, 2022. https://lunarspell.
com/blog/runic-magic/

Lin, Kimberly. (2017, March 21). "Edda." WorldHistory.org.
Accessed January 12th, 2022. https://www.
worldhistory.org/Edda/

Manea, Irina-Maria. (2021, February 23). "Viking Prophecy: The
Poem Völuspá of the Poetic Edda." World History Encyclopedia.
Accessed January 30th, 2022. https://www.worldhistory.org/
article/1674/viking-prophecy-the-poem-voluspa-of-the-poetic-edd/

Mark, Joshua J. (2019, January 10). "Norse-Viking Symbols &

Meanings." WorldHistory.org. Accessed January 23rd, 2022. https://www.worldhistory.org/article/1309/norse-viking-symbols--meanings/

McCoy, Daniel. (n.d.a). "Cosmology." Norse Mythology for Smart People. Accessed January 12th, 2022. https://norse-mythology.org/cosmology/

McCoy, Daniel. (n.d.b). "Gods and Creatures." Norse Mythology for Smart People. Accessed January 12th, 2022. https://norse-mythology.org/gods-and-creatures/

McCoy, Daniel. (n.d.c). "The Helm of Awe." Norse Mythology for Smart People. Accessed January 12th, 2022. https://norse-mythology.org/symbols/helm-of-awe/

McCoy, Daniel. (n.d.d). "Magic" Norse Mythology for Smart People. Accessed January 12th, 2022. https://norse-mythology.org/concepts/magic/

McCoy, Daniel. (n.d.e). "The Meanings of the Runes." Norse Mythology for Smart People. Accessed January 12th, 2022. https://norse-mythology.org/runes/the-meanings-of-the-runes/

McCoy, Daniel. (n.d.f). "Norse Theology." Norse Mythology for Smart People. Accessed January 12th, 2022. https://norse-mythology.org/concepts/polytheistic-theology-and-ethics/

McCoy, Daniel. (n.d.g). "The Origins of the Runes." Norse Mythology for Smart People. Accessed January 12th, 2022. https://norse-mythology.org/runes/the-origins-of-the-runes/

McCoy, Daniel. (n.d.h). "Runes." Norse Mythology for Smart

People. Accessed January 12th, 2022. https://norse-mythology.org/runes/

McCoy, Daniel. (n.d.i). "Runic Philosophy and Magic." Norse Mythology for Smart People. Accessed January 12th, 2022. https://norse-mythology.org/runes/runic-philosophy-and-magic/

McCoy, Daniel. (n.d.j). "Seidr." Norse Mythology for Smart People. Accessed January 12th, 2022. https://norse-mythology.org/concepts/seidr/

McCoy, Daniel. (n.d.k). "The Svefnthorn." Norse Mythology for Smart People. Accessed January 12th, 2022. https://norse-mythology.org/symbols/svefnthorn/

McKay, Andrew. (2021, March 9). "Viking Runes: The Historic Writing Systems of Northern Europe." LifeInNorway.net. Accessed January 28, 2022. https://www.lifeinnorway.net/viking-runes/

Merriam-Webster. (n.d.). "Venerate." Merriam-Webster.com. Accessed January 24th, 2022. https://www.merriam-webster.com/dictionary/venerate

Metcalfe, Tom. (2020, October 8). "1,200-year-old pagan temple to Thor and Odin unearthed in Norway." LiveScience. Accessed January 12th, 2022. https://www.livescience.com/ancient-viking-temple-to-thor-odin-unearthed.html

Näsström, B.-M. (1999, February 1). Fragments of the past: how to study old Norse religion. *Scripta Instituti Donneriani Aboensis*, *17*(2). Accessed January 11th, 2022. https://doi.org/10.30674/scripta.67271

National Museum of Denmark. (n.d.a). "The gods of the old Nordic religion." National Museum of Denmark Website. Accessed January 11th, 2022. https://en.natmus.dk/historical-knowledge/denmark/prehistoric-period-until-1050-ad/the-viking-age/religion-magic-death-and-rituals/the-viking-gods/

National Museum of Denmark. (n.d.b). "Human sacrifices?" National Museum of Denmark Website. Accessed January 11th, 2022. https://en.natmus.dk/historical-knowledge/denmark/prehistoric-period-until-1050-ad/the-viking-age/religion-magic-death-and-rituals/human-sacrifices/

National Museum of Denmark. (n.d.c). "The magic wands of Viking seeresses?" National Museum of Denmark Website. Accessed January 11th, 2022. https://en.natmus.dk/historical-knowledge/denmark/prehistoric-period-until-1050-ad/the-viking-age/religion-magic-death-and-rituals/the-magic-wands-of-the-seeresses/

National Museum of Denmark. (n.d.d). "The old Nordic religion today." National Museum of Denmark Website. Accessed January 11th, 2022. https://en.natmus.dk/historical-knowledge/denmark/prehistoric-period-until-1050-ad/the-viking-age/religion-magic-death-and-rituals/the-old-nordic-religion-today/

National Museum of Denmark. (n.d.e). "The old religion." National Museum of Denmark Website. Accessed January 11th, 2022. https://en.natmus.dk/historical-knowledge/denmark/prehistoric-period-until-1050-ad/the-viking-age/religion-magic-death-and-rituals/the-old-religion/

National Museum of Denmark. (n.d.f). "Runic magic." National Museum of Denmark Website. Accessed January 11th, 2022. https://en.natmus.dk/historical-knowledge/denmark/prehistoric-period-until-1050-ad/the-viking-age/religion-magic-death-and-rituals/runic-magic/

National Museum of Denmark. (n.d.g). "A seeress from Fyrkat?" National Museum of Denmark Website. Accessed January 11th, 2022. https://en.natmus.dk/historical-knowledge/denmark/prehistoric-period-until-1050-ad/the-viking-age/religion-magic-death-and-rituals/a-seeress-from-fyrkat/

National Museum of Denmark. (n.d.h). "The seeresses of the Viking period." National Museum of Denmark Website. Accessed January 11th, 2022. https://en.natmus.dk/historical-knowledge/denmark/prehistoric-period-until-1050-ad/the-viking-age/religion-magic-death-and-rituals/viking-seeresses/

National Museum of Denmark. (n.d.i). "The Viking blót sacrifices." National Museum of Denmark Website. Accessed January 11th, 2022. https://en.natmus.dk/historical-knowledge/denmark/prehistoric-period-until-1050-ad/the-viking-age/religion-magic-death-and-rituals/the-viking-blot-sacrifices

Nikel, David. (2020, May 15). "Scandinavian Runestones: Viking History in Plain Sight." LifeInNorway.net. Accessed January 29th, 2022. https://www.lifeinnorway.net/scandinavian-runestones/

Parker, Sam. (2015, June 18). "World's first modern-day pagan temple is in Newark." Newark Advertiser. Accessed January 17th, 2022. https://www.newarkadvertiser.co.uk/news/sn9xmbrejj4nkkzhufy4ykh0vstjmto37onp1d7fxki6y-9036836/

Reese, W. L. (2000, August 25). "Pantheism." Encyclopedia Britannica. Accessed January 12th, 2022. https://www.britannica.com/topic/pantheism

Rogador, Christine. (2020a, August 24). "Mjölnir Symbol – History and Meaning." SymbolsArchive.com. Accessed January 23rd, 2022. https://symbolsarchive.com/mjolnir-symbol/

Rogador, Christine. (2020b, August 24). "The Triple Horn of Odin Symbol – History And Meaning." SymbolsArchive.com. Accessed January 23rd, 2022. https://symbolsarchive.com/triple-horn-of-odin-symbol-history-meaning/

Rogador, Christine. (2020c, September 17). "Gungnir Symbol – History And Meaning." SymbolsArchive.com. Accessed January 24th, 2022. https://symbolsarchive.com/gungnir-symbol-history-meaning/

Rogador, Christine. (2021, April 12). "Viking Symbols And Their Meaning." SymbolsArchive.com. Accessed January 24th, 2022. https://symbolsarchive.com/viking-symbols-and-their-meaning/

Scott, Jess. (2021, October 8). "A Beginner's Guide to Norse Mythology." LifeInNorway.net. Accessed January 13th, 2022. https://www.lifeinnorway.net/norse-mythology/

Short, William R. (n.d.) "Pagan Religious Practices of the Viking Age." Hurstwic.org. Accessed January 12th, 2022. http://www.hurstwic.org/history/articles/mythology/religion/text/practices.htm

Siofra. (2021, December). "The 3 Aettirs of the Elder Futhark." Spells8.com. Accessed January 25th, 2022. https://forum.spells8.com/t/the-3-aettirs-of-the-elder-futhark/17330

Staff, Iceland Magazine. (2019, January 22). "11 things to know about the present day practice of Ásatrú, the ancient religion of the Vikings." Iceland Magazine. Accessed January 19th, 2022.

https://icelandmag.is/article/11-things-know-about-present-day-practice-asatru-ancient-religion-vikings

Time Nomads. (2021, October 8). "Norse Paganism for Beginners: Quick Recap + Resources." TimeNomads.com. Accessed January 19th, 2022. https://www.timenomads.com/norse-paganism-for-beginners/

Time Nomads. (2021a, October 8). "Rune Magic 101: What are and How to Make Bind Runes." TimeNomads.com. Accessed January 30th, 2022. https://www.timenomads.com/rune-magic-101-what-are-and-how-to-make-norse-bind-runes/

Time Nomads. (2021b, October 8). "How to Make Your Own Rune Set." TimeNomads.com. Accessed January 30th, 2022. https://www.timenomads.com/how-to-make-your-own-rune-set/

Traylor, Dean. (2019, December 15). "Huginn and Munnin: The Divine Ravens of Odin." Owlcation.com. Accessed January 24th, 2022. https://owlcation.com/humanities/Huginn-and-Muninn-As-The-Divine-Ravens-of-Odin

Turville-Petre, E. and Polomé, Edgar Charles (2006, June 9). "Germanic religion and mythology." Encyclopedia Britannica. Accessed January 12th, 2022. https://www.britannica.com/topic/Germanic-religion-and-mythology

Vickers, Mark R. (2020, October 11). "On the Complexities and Mysteries of Norse Magic." TheTollkeeper.com. Accessed January 22, 2022. http://thetollkeeper.com/2020/10/11/on-the-complexities-and-mysteries-of-norse-magic/

Viking Answer Lady. (n.d.) "Women and Magic in the Sagas: Seiðr

and Spá." VikingAnswerLady.com. Accessed January 30th, 2022.
http://www.vikinganswerlady.com/seidhr.shtml

Wigington, Patti. (2019b, July 5). "Asatru - Norse Heathens of
Modern Paganism." LearnReligions.com. Accessed January 19th,
2022. https://www.learnreligions.com/asatru-modern-paganism-
2562545

Wigington, Patti. (2019a, July 31). "Magical Pagan and Wiccan
Symbols." LearnReligions.com. Accessed January 17th, 2022.
https://www.learnreligions.com/pagan-and-wiccan-symbols-
4123036

Wigington, Patti. (2018b, December 10). "The Nine Noble
Virtues of Asatru." LearnReligions.com. Accessed January 19th,
2022. https://www.learnreligions.com/noble-virtues-of-asatru-
2561539

Wigington, Patti. (2019, March 28). "Norse Deities." LearnReli-
gions.com. Accessed January 14th, 2022. https://www.
learnreligions.com/norse-deities-4590158

Wigington, Patti. (2018, February 28). "The Norse Eddas and
Sagas." LearnReligions.com. Accessed January 12th, 2022. https://
www.learnreligions.com/norse-eddas-and-sagas-2561561

Wigington, Patti. (2019c, March 31). "The Norse Runes - A Basic
Overview." LearnReligions.com. Accessed January 28th, 2022.
https://www.learnreligions.com/norse-runes-basic-overview-
2562815

Wigington, Patti. (2020, January 31). "What Is Rune Casting?
Origins and Techniques." LearnReligions.com. Accessed January

30th, 2022. https://www.learnreligions.com/rune-casting-4783609

Wilkes, Jonny. (2021, November 18). "Gods, myths and rituals: what we know about Viking religious beliefs." BBC History Extra. Accessed January 12th, 2022. https://www.historyextra.com/period/viking/viking-religion-gods-myths-rituals-ship-burial-sacrifice-odin-thor-loki/

Woolf, Jo. (2016, April 14). "Tree Folklore: Birch, the Lady of the Wood." FolkloreThursday.com. Accessed January 30th, 2022. https://folklorethursday.com/myths/birch-lady-wood/

Wright, Mackenzie Sage. (2020, July 9). "Wicca for Beginners: What Are Grounding and Centering, and How Do You Do Them?" Exemplore.com. Accessed January 25th, 2022. https://exemplore.com/wicca-witchcraft/Wicca-for-Beginners-What-are-Grounding-and-Centering-and-How-Do-You-Do-Them

www.ingramcontent.com/pod-product-compliance
Lightning Source LLC
Chambersburg PA
CBHW051002140626
46546CB00017B/2398